D1785181

Article 4

The Nature of States Parties' Obligations

A Commentary on the United Nations Convention
on the Rights of the Child

Editors

André Alen, Johan Vande Lanotte, Eugeen Verhellen,
Fiona Ang, Eva Berghmans and Mieke Verheyde

Article 4

The Nature of States Parties' Obligations

By

Mervat Rishmawi

Legal Advisor

MARTINUS NIJHOFF PUBLISHERS
LEIDEN • BOSTON
2006

This book is printed on acid-free paper.

A Cataloging-in-Publication record for this book is available from the Library of Congress.

Cite as: M. Rishmawi, "Article 4: The Nature of States Parties' Obligations", in: A. Alen, J. Vande Lanotte, E. Verhellen, F. Ang, E. Berghmans, M. Verheyde (Eds.) *A Commentary on the United Nations Convention on the Rights of the Child* (Martinus Nijhoff Publishers, Leiden, 2006).

ISSN 1574-8626
ISBN 90-04-14708-X

© 2006 by Koninklijke Brill NV, Leiden, The Netherlands.
Koninklijke Brill NV incorporates the imprints Brill Academic Publishers,
Martinus Nijhoff Publishers and VSP.

Cover image by Nadia, 1 $^1/_2$ years old.

http://www.brill.nl

All rights reserved. No part of this publication may be reproduced, translated, stored in a retrieval system, or transmitted in any form or by any means, electronic, mechanical, photo-copying, recording or otherwise, without prior written permission from the publisher.

Authorization to photocopy items for internal or personal use is granted by Brill provided that the appropriate fees are paid directly to The Copyright Clearance Center, 222 Rosewood Drive, Suite 910, Danvers, MA 01923, USA.
Fees are subject to change.

PRINTED IN THE NETHERLANDS

CONTENTS

LIST OF ABBREVIATIONS

CESCR Committee	Committee on Economic, Social and Cultural Rights
CRC	Convention on the Rights of the Child
CRC Committee	Committee on the Rights of the Child
CEDAW Committee	Committee on Elimination of All Forms of Discrimination against Women
CAT	Convention against Torture and Other Cruel, Inhuman or Degrading Treatment or Punishment
GNP	Gross National Product
HIPC	Heavily Indebted Poor Countries initiative
CESCR	International Covenant on Economic, Social and Cultural Rights
CCPR	International Covenant on Civil and Political Rights
CEDAW	International Convention on the Elimination of All Forms of Discrimination against Women
CERD	International Convention on the Elimination of All Forms of Racial Discrimination
ICRC	International Committee of the Red Cross
IMF	International Monetary Fund
MDGs	Millennium Development Goals
PRSPs	Poverty Reduction Strategy Papers
SAPs	Structural Adjustment Programs
UNICEF	United Nations Children's Fund
UNDP	United Nations Development Program

AUTHOR BIOGRAPHY

Mervant Rishmawi holds an LLM in International Human Rights Law from the University of Essex. She is currently Acting Deputy Director for the Middle East and North Africa Programme at the International Secretariat of Amnesty International and is the Legal Advisor to the same region at AI.* During this period, she maintains overview responsibility in the Legal and International Organisations Program for children's rights and economic, social and cultural rights. Previously she coordinated campaigns in the Middle East and North Africa Program for Amnesty International. She has also been part of the first Team to Implement the Plan of Action to Strengthen the Implementation of the Convention on the Rights of the Child in the UN Office of the High Commissioner for Human Rights. Prior to that, Mervat Rishmawi worked in Palestine with al-Haq, the West Bank affiliate for the International Commission of Jurists, as a researcher, coordinator of the Field-Work Unit, and coordinator of the Legal Services Unit. She was also involved with a number of NGOs in Palestine including those working on children's rights and workers' rights. Mervat Rishmawi acted as a consultant to many UN specialised agencies, including the ILO and UNICEF. She is also active in the human rights movement in the Middle East and North Africa.

---

* This document is written in a personal capacity and does not necessarily reflect the views and positions of Amnesty International on the subject.

TEXT OF ARTICLE 4

ARTICLE 4

'States Parties shall undertake all appropriate legislative, administrative, and other measures for the implementation of the rights recognized in the present Convention. With regard to economic, social and cultural rights, States Parties shall undertake such measures to the maximum extent of their available resources and, where needed, within the framework of international co-operation.'

ARTICLE 4

'Les Etats parties s'engagent à prendre toutes les mesures législatives, administratives et autres qui sont nécessaires pour mettre en oeuvre les droits reconnus dans la présente Convention. Dans le cas des droits économiques, sociaux et culturels, ils prennent ces mesures dans toutes les limites des ressources dont ils disposent et, s'il y a lieu, dans le cadre de la coopération internationale.'

CHAPTER ONE

INTRODUCTION*

1. Article 4 of the Convention on the Rights of the Child (CRC) concerns the nature of States Parties' obligations. It consists of three important elements. Firstly, it addresses the obligation of States Parties to take 'all appropriate legislative, administrative, and other measures for the implementation of the rights recognized in the . . . Convention.' Secondly, the Convention makes a distinction in terms of the measures to be taken in relation to economic, social, and cultural rights, providing that States Parties 'shall undertake such measures to the maximum extent of their available resources'. Thirdly, and connected to that, Article 4 states that where needed, the progressive nature of the implementation of economic, social and cultural rights should be undertaken within the framework of international co-operation.

2. Each of these three elements is examined here in the light of the drafting history of the Convention. The reporting guidelines related to Article 4 as set out by the CRC Committee are used as a basis, together with evidence drawn from concluding observations, the majority of which date from the last three years.[1] Reference to relevant general comments by the CRC Committee and other treaty bodies is also included. UN documents including declarations and plans of actions that relate to children are used to demonstrate different aspects of State obligations. Court judgments at the national, regional and international levels are used to elaborate and illustrate various points. Finally, previous work by other colleagues and scholars in this field, as well as work and documents by UN specialized agencies is also cited where relevant.

---

* February 2005. A major part of the preliminary research for this document was carried out by my colleague Carlos Gaio. His thorough and creative research and ideas were of tremendous assistance to me. This document could not have been written without him. The insightful comments I received from Iain Byrne were very valuable for the development of the ideas in this document. I am very grateful to him.

[1] A thorough discussion of the CRC Committee's concluding observations during the first 9 years (150 initial and second reports), together with other key comments by other treaty bodies, is included in R. Hodgkin and P. Newell, *Implementation Handbook for the Convention of the Rights of the Child* (New York/Geneva, UNICEF, 2002), 762 p. This document relies on it and complements it with concluding observations that were issued after that publication.

3. To understand Article 4 in a comprehensive way, it is important to examine aspects that are directly related to the different elements of the Article. These include a comparison between the Article and other similar provisions in regional and international instruments, as well as considering specifically the similarity between the CRC and the two Covenants, and between Article 4 and other articles in the CRC. This includes a discussion of the nature of legislative and administrative measures, and what needs to be taken into account when discussing resource allocation. There is a brief discussion of international co-operation and foreign debt, including international aid, the role of the World Bank and the IMF, and the Eight Millennium Development Goals. Finally, a discussion of the nature of States Parties' obligations would not be complete without a discussion on reservations and restrictions of rights according to the CRC. The document ends with a brief overview of issues related to implementation including the need for systematic review and evaluation, ensuring effective remedies, and defining what constitutes a violation through the use of data and indicators.

4. The aim of this document is to explore in detail the normative aspect of Article 4 by analyzing in depth the recommendations of the CRC Committee, together with other relevant bodies. It is hoped that this will help policy makers, jurists, service providers and members of NGOs to identify policies and prioritize steps that need to be taken to implement the principles and provisions of the CRC in the light of Article 4.

5. Given that Article 4 necessarily relates to most of the other provisions of the CRC, reference is made on occasions to some of these other provisions. However, discussion of the substantive nature of these rights is not addressed in this document.

CHAPTER TWO

COMPARISON WITH RELATED INTERNATIONAL
HUMAN RIGHTS PROVISIONS

6. The CRC includes civil, political, economic, social and cultural rights in one document.[2] Parts of Article 4 are therefore similar to the wording of those in international treaties covering either set of rights in relation to the nature of State obligations.

1. *Universal Instruments*

7. The international instruments reviewed in this section are the main international human rights treaties which have particular relevance to the protection of children's rights and contain some provisions similar to a certain degree to those in the CRC dealing with the same issues. They all contain a provision defining the nature of States Parties' obligations, similar to that of Article 4 of the CRC. The international instruments covered in this section are: the International Covenant on Civil and Political Rights (CCPR), the International Covenant on Economic, Social and Cultural Rights (CESCR), the Convention against Torture and Other Cruel, Inhuman or Degrading Treatment or Punishment (CAT), the International Convention on the Elimination of All Forms of Racial Discrimination (CERD), and the International Convention on the Elimination of All Forms of Discrimination against Women (CEDAW).[3] It is important to study the similarities or differences between these instruments and the CRC in relation to States Parties' obligations in order to ascertain the possible impact of the differences on protection of children's rights.

---

[2] The CRC does not include some rights that traditionally are seen to be of concern to adults but do not relate to children, for example in relation to some aspects of political participation, including to be elected to public office, or possibly the right to form and join trade unions.

[3] CCPR was adopted by General Assembly resolution 2200 A (XXI) of 16 December 1966, CESCR was adopted by General Assembly resolution 2200 A (XXI) of 16 December 1966, CAT was adopted by General Assembly resolution 39/46 of 10 December 1984, CERD was adopted by General Assembly resolution 2106 A (XX) of 21 December 1965, and CEDAW was adopted by General Assembly resolution 34/80 of 18 December 1979.

8. The International Convention on the Protection of the Rights of All Migrant Workers and Members of Their Families does not include a provision in its first six parts that relate to definitions, scope and rights, similar to those mentioned above in relation to measures of implementation.[4] However, the seventh part of the Convention, which deals with implementation and reporting to the Committee established to review reports on implementation of the Convention, requires States to report on 'legislative, judicial, administrative and other measures' (Article 73 (1)).

1.1   *Legislative, Administrative and Other Measures*

9. The first sentence of Article 4 of the CRC provides that '[S]tates Parties shall undertake all appropriate legislative, administrative, and other measures for the implementation of the rights recognized in the present Convention.' This is largely similar to Article 2 (2) of the CCPR which states:

> 'Where not already provided for by existing legislative or other measures, each State Party to the present Covenant undertakes to take the necessary steps, in accordance with its constitutional processes and with the provisions of the present Covenant, to adopt such laws or other measures as may be necessary to give effect to the rights recognized in the present Covenant.'

10. The CCPR provision uses the formulation 'legislative or other measures' in one instant, and 'laws and other measures' in another and does not include specific mention of administrative measures. The CRC, on the other hand, uses the formulation 'legislative, administrative and other measures'. As will be discussed later, the formula used in the CRC is meant to be inclusive of any measures that should be taken to implement the Convention. The use of 'other measures' in the CRC is to ensure consistency of the CRC with other international human rights instruments, and the consistency of Article 4 with subsequent articles in the Convention, which often specify other measures that go beyond legislation.[5] Further, while the CCPR states that steps should be taken in accordance with the constitutional process, the CRC does not include this qualification. It is understood, however, that the reference to 'appropriate' measures is to include consideration of those

---

[4] Adopted by General Assembly resolution 45/158 of 18 December 1990.
[5] See Comment by UNICEF during the drafting of the CRC, contained in E/CN.4/1989/WG.1/ CPR.1, 1989, pp. 17–20, reproduced in *Legislative History of the Convention of the Rights of the Child (1978-1989), Article 4 (Implementation of Rights)*, contained in UN Doc. HR/1995/Ser.1/article. 4, p. 11. This document is a compilation of all relevant official documents of the drafting history of the Convention on the Rights of the Child, as prepared by the UN Centre for Human Rights.

provided by the constitution.[6] The CRC is therefore wider in scope and allows for measures to be adopted in any way that the national system requires as long as it fulfils the requirements of Article 4 of the CRC in relation to the nature of States Parties' obligations.

11. The CESCR uses the formulation 'in all appropriate means, including particularly the adoption of legislative measures.' The Limburg Principles on the Implementation of the International Covenant on Economic, Social and Cultural Rights (the Limburg Principles) clearly states that it is the responsibility of the States 'to use all appropriate means, including legislative, administrative, judicial, economic, social and educational measures' in order to fulfil the obligations under the CESCR. The Principles clarify further that legislative measures alone are not sufficient. Appropriate remedies, including when applicable judicial remedies, should also be provided.[7]

12. CAT uses similar wording in Article 2(1) to the CRC as it places an obligation on each State Party to 'take effective legislative, administrative, judicial or other measures to prevent acts of torture in any territory under its jurisdiction.' The inclusion of 'judicial' measures in CAT emphasizes the need for such measures to prevent and combat torture.

13. CERD on the other hand, states that '[e]ach State Party shall take effective measures to review governmental, national and local policies, and to amend, rescind or nullify any laws and regulations which have the effect of creating or perpetuating racial discrimination wherever it exists' (Article 2 (1 (c)). This specific requirement to review policies regularly is one of the measures that the CRC Committee emphasizes regularly in its concluding observations and in its reporting guidelines, as will be discussed later. This reflects that, although it is not explicit in the CRC as a general measure, the CRC Committee believes that this is paramount for the protection of children's rights. CERD is a very important instrument that elaborates on protection from racial discrimination. Although the CRC includes some provisions relevant in this regard (for example Article 30 of the CRC), it does not include an elaboration on this. Therefore, the details of the nature of States Parties' obligations according to CERD is relevant to the CRC, and could be regarded as further guidance to understand Article 4 of the CRC.

---

[6] See S. Detrick, *A Commentary on the United Nations Convention on the Rights of the Child* (The Hague/Boston/London, Martinus Nijhoff Publishers, 1999), p. 104.

[7] The Limburg Principles on the Implementation of the International Covenant on Economic, Social and Cultural Rights of 6 June 1986, (UN Doc. E/CN.4/1987/17, 1987); reproduced in *Human Rights Quarterly* 9, 1987, pp. 122–135; principles 17, 18 and 19.

14. CEDAW adopts a similar approach to CERD, but breaks down the measures in more details. It states in Article 2 that States Parties 'agree to pursue by all appropriate means and without delay a policy of eliminating discrimination against women'. As with CERD, this detailed list of implementation offers helpful guidance for the implementation of the CRC. Many of these are included in specific concluding observations by the CRC in its General Comment No. 5 on General Measures of Implementation of the CRC.

15. The Maastricht Guidelines on Violations of Economic, Social and Cultural Rights (the Maastricht Guidelines), elaborate a violations approach to economic, social and cultural rights generally and not just to the CESCR.[8] They clarify that these rights, like civil and political rights, impose obligations to respect, protect and fulfil.[9] Each of these obligations includes elements of obligation of conduct and of result, and these occur through acts of omission and acts of commission.[10] In relation to legislative measures related to economic, social and cultural rights, the Guidelines clarify that the violation through acts of omission occurs through, for example, the removal of legislation that is *necessary* for the continued enjoyment of economic, social and cultural rights; or through the adoption of legislation or policies which are manifestly incompatible with pre-existing legal obligations.[11] This Guideline should have been wider to prohibit adoptions of laws and policies that reduce the enjoyment of rights or are in violation of provisions and principles of international law, including the prohibition of discrimination, or the obligation to increase equality, for example.[12] Similarly, violations through acts of omission occur through the failure to reform or repeal existing legislation.[13]

1.2   *Resource Allocation and International Co-operation*

16. The second sentence of Article 4 of the CRC states: '[w]ith regard to economic, social and cultural rights, States Parties shall undertake such measures to the maximum extent of their available resources and, where

---

[8] Maastricht Guidelines on Violations of Economic, Social and Cultural Rights (UN Doc. E/C.12/2000/13, 2000), reproduced in *Human Rights Quarterly* 20, 1998, pp. 691–705, Guideline 3.
[9] Maastricht Guidelines, Guideline 6.
[10] Maastricht Guidelines, Guideline 7.
[11] Maastricht Guidelines, Guideline 14 (a) and (d).
[12] See V. Dankwa, C. Flinterman, and S. Leckie, 'Commentary to the Maastricht Guidelines on Violations of Economic, Social and Cultural Rights', *Human Rights Quarterly* 20, 1998, p. 720.
[13] Maastricht Guidelines, Guideline 15 (b).

needed, within the framework of international co-operation.' This is largely similar to Article 2 (1) of the CESCR which states:

> 'Each State Party to the present Covenant undertakes to take steps, individually and through international assistance and co-operation, especially economic and technical, to the maximum of its available resources, with a view to achieving progressively the full realization of the rights recognized in the present Covenant by all appropriate means, including particularly the adoption of legislative measures.'

17. However, the provision in the CESCR is more explicit than that of the CRC. It requires States to undertake steps to the maximum of their available resources, with the view to achieving progressively the full realization of the rights. Whilst the CRC includes the same wording on the maximum available resources, the aim of achieving *the full realization* of the rights is not explicitly included. Further, while international co-operation in the CRC is stated in general terms, the CESCR makes this more specific and refers to steps taken individually and through international co-operation, and further specifies that this type of assistance or co-operation can especially be economic and technical. The third chapter below will elaborate further on these aspects.

18. CERD, in addressing economic, social and cultural rights, does not include a similar reference to progressive realization of the rights and technical assistance. It states in Article 2 (2) that 'in the social, economic, cultural and other fields, [States Parties shall take] special and concrete measures to ensure the adequate development and protection of certain racial groups or individuals belonging to them, for the purpose of guaranteeing them the full and equal enjoyment of human rights and fundamental freedoms.' Article 3 of the CEDAW states that: 'States Parties shall take in all fields, in particular in the political, social, economic and cultural fields, all appropriate measures, including legislation, to ensure the full development and advancement of women, for the purpose of guaranteeing them the exercise and enjoyment of human rights and fundamental freedoms on a basis of equality with men'. These two instruments are relevant to children for example in relation to protection from racial discrimination in the case of CERD, and in relation to rights of the girl child in the case of CEDAW. As will be discussed later, during the drafting of the CRC, the fact that these two instruments do not allow for progressive realization of the rights was made to illustrate that not all the rights – especially civil and political rights – should be subject to progressive realization.

2. Regional Instruments

19. This section discusses provisions in the regional instruments of the Inter-American, African and European systems related to Article 4 of the CRC. The Arab Charter on Human Rights, adopted by the League of Arab States in 1994, has been re-drafted and adopted again by the Summit of the League of Arab States in June 2004.[14] The previous version of the Arab Charter falls short of international human rights standards in many aspects and has been widely criticised by NGOs. It also has not yet been ratified and thus did not enter into force. The Charter does not include a provision on measures of implementation. For these reasons, it is not discussed here. The new version of the Arab Charter incorporates guarantees for rights that are largely consistent with international human rights, including many rights of the child. However, many parts of the current Charter remain of concern to many NGOs.[15] Beyond the non-discrimination clause which states that a 'State Party to the present Charter undertakes to ensure to all individuals subject to its jurisdiction the right to enjoy the rights and freedoms set forth herein, without distinction', the Charter does not include a specific provision on the nature of States Parties' obligations.

2.1 Legislative, Administrative and Other Measures

20. The *American Convention on Human Rights* (known as Pact of San Jose) states:[16]

'Where the exercise of any of the rights or freedoms referred to in Article 1 is not already ensured by legislative or other provisions, the States Parties

---

[14] The re-drafted Arab Charter on Human Rights, was adopted during the Summit of the League of Arab States in May 2004. The original Charter on Human Rights was adopted in 1994, but did not receive any ratification. The new Arab Charter on Human Rights has, by the end of January 2005, been ratified by Jordan only. The redrafting of the Arab Charter on Human Rights was based on the Decision 6355 of the Council of the League of Arab States in its 120th session, of 9 September 2003.

[15] For further discussion on the Arab Charter on Human Rights see Amnesty International, *Middle East and North Africa Region: Re-drafting the Arab Charter on Human Rights: Building for a better future* (AI Index: MDE 01/002/2004, 11 March 2004). See also *Second Independence: Towards an Initiative for Political Reform in the Arab World: The recommendations of the First Civil Forum Parallel to the Arab Summit* (Beirut 19–22 March 2004).

[16] American Convention on Human Rights, O.A.S. Treaty Series No. 36, 1144 U.N.T.S. 123 entered into force July 18, 1978, reprinted in *Basic Documents Pertaining to Human Rights in the Inter-American System*, OEA/Ser.L.V/II.82 doc.6 rev.1 at 25 (1992).

undertake to adopt, in accordance with their constitutional processes and the provisions of this Convention, such legislative or other measures as may be necessary to give effect to those rights or freedoms.'

21. The formulation adopted here is similar to that in the CCPR, which includes the requirement to take steps in accordance with constitutional processes. While the CRC does not include this specific formulation, as discussed above, it is understood that the reference to appropriate measures in Article 4 of the CRC is to include this (see above under Universal Instruments).

22. Elaboration of the nature of States Parties' obligations according to the Convention is seen through Articles 1 and 2. Article 1 requires States Parties to respect, ensure, investigate and sanction violations, and imposes the duty to make reparations for violations of rights in the Convention. This is further elaborated in Article 2 which requires States to ensure domestic legal effect of the Convention. It is argued that, on the basis of the findings of the Inter-American Commission on Human Rights and the American Court on Human Rights, the duty to ensure includes the duty to prevent, regulate, monitor, conduct impact studies, and the duty to remove structural obstacles.[17]

23. The *European Convention on Human Rights*[18] does not include provisions similar to those in the other international or regional treaties relating to the nature of States Parties' obligations. This has been clarified mainly through judgments of the European Court on Human Rights, which emphasized a number of obligations. The Court has repeatedly emphasized and developed positive obligations, which require States to take a number of actions ranging from omission of violations, to investigation of violations, protection of the right, and to provide redress within a reasonable period of time, for example.[19] It should be highlighted that the Court also sees that there is a positive obligation on the State to protect rights in the private lives.[20] Further, the Court said:

---

[17] For a discussion on the nature of in the inter-American system see T. Melish, *Protecting Economic, Social and Cultural Rights in the Inter-American Human Rights System: A Manual on Presenting Claims* (Ecuador, Orville H. Schell Jr. Centre for International Human Rights, Yale Law School and Centro de Derechos Económicos y Sociales, 2002), pp. 155-192.

[18] Convention on the Protection of Human Rights and Fundamental Freedoms, 213 U.N.T.S. 222, entered into force 3 September 1953, as amended by Protocols Nos. 3, 5, 8, and 11, which entered into force on 21 September 1970, 20 December 1971, 1 January 1990, and 1 November 1998 respectively.

[19] For a detailed discussion on positive obligations, see A. Mowbray, *The development of positive obligations under the European Convention on Human Rights by the European Court of Human Rights* (Oxford, Hart Publishers, 2004), 255 p.

[20] ECtHR, *Osman v. United Kingdom*, 28 October 1998, No. 23452/94, *Reports 1998-VIII*, especially para. 115.

'The political and institutional organisation of the Member States must accordingly respect the rights and principles enshrined in the Convention. It matters little in this context whether the provisions in issue are constitutional (see, for example, the Gitonas and Others v. Greece judgment of 1 July 1997, Reports of Judgments and Decisions 1997-IV) or merely legislative (see, for example, the Mathieu-Mohin and Clerfayt v. Belgium judgment of 2 March 1987, Series A no. 113). From the moment that such provisions are the means by which the State concerned exercises its jurisdiction, they are subject to review under the Convention.'[21]

24. Further, the Court stated in another case that:

'Eliminating what are judged to be social injustices is an example of the functions of a democratic legislature. More especially, modern societies consider housing of the population to be a prime social need, the regulation of which cannot entirely be left to the play of market forces. The margin of appreciation is wide enough to cover legislation aimed at securing greater social justice in the sphere of people's homes, even where such legislation interferes with existing contractual relations between private parties and confers no direct benefit on the State or the community at large.'[22]

25. It is therefore clear from this that the Court envisages that the State, in the interests of social justice, should both implement legislative measures and be prepared to intervene in the affairs of private actors.

26. In relation to economic, social and cultural rights, the 'Court is aware that the further realization of social and economic rights is largely dependent on the situation – notably financial – reigning the State in question'. The Court adds: 'Whilst the Convention sets forth what are essentially civil and political rights, many of them have implications of a social or economic nature.'[23]

27. Article 1 (1) of the *African Charter on the Rights and Welfare of the Child*[24] (ACRWC) defines the nature of State obligations:

'Member States of the Organization of African Unity, Parties to the present Charter shall recognize the rights, freedoms and duties enshrined in this Charter and shall undertake the necessary steps, in accordance with their

---

[21] ECtHR, *The United Communist Party of Turkey and Others v. Turkey*, 30 January 1998, No. 19392/92, *Reports 1998-I*, para. 30.

[22] ECtHR, *James and Others v. United Kingdom*, 21 February 1986, No. 8793/79, *Publications of the Court*, A98, para. 47.

[23] ECtHR, *Airey v. Ireland*, 9 October 1979, No. 6289/73, *Publications of the Court*, A32, para. 26.

[24] Adopted by the Organization of African Unity in 1990 (OAU Doc. CAB/LEG/24.9/49).

constitutional processes and with the provisions of the present Charter, to adopt such legislative or other measures as may be necessary to give effect to the provisions of this Charter.'

28. It is interesting that, although the Charter is a catalogue of rights and freedoms largely similar to the CRC, it does not have a specific provision qualifying the nature of State obligations in relation to economic, social or cultural rights. The African Committee on the Rights of the Child is a newly established committee and therefore there is to date no jurisprudence by it elaborating the nature of State obligations.

29. Article 1 of the *African Charter on Human and Peoples' Rights*[25] states:

'The Member States of the Organization of African Unity, Parties to the present Charter shall recognize the rights, duties and freedoms enshrined in this Chapter and shall undertake to adopt legislative or other measures to give effect to them.'

30. This is similar to the formulation used in the CRC in relation to legislative and other measures. The jurisprudence of the African Court on Human Rights and the African Commission on Human Rights reflect that States are under the obligation to enact legislation at the national and municipal level. It also emphasizes the full participation in government, and measures of awareness raising of rights, and especially of training government officials.[26]

2.2   Resource Allocation and International Co-Operation

31. Article 26 of the *American Convention on Human Rights* addresses specifically economic, social and cultural rights stating:

'The States Parties undertake to adopt measures, both internally and through international co-operation, especially those of an economic and technical nature, with a view to achieving progressively, by legislation or other appropriate means, the full realization of the rights implicit in the economic, social, educational, scientific, and cultural standards set forth in the Charter of the Organization of American States as amended by the Protocol of Buenos Aires.'

32. The *Protocol of San Salvador*[27] is the Additional Protocol to the American Convention on Human rights in the area of Economic, Social and Cultural

---

[25] Adopted by the Organization of African Unity, (OAU Doc. CAB/LEG/67/3 rev. 5, 21 I.L.M. 58 (1982), 27 June 1981.

[26] For further analysis of the subject, see U.O. Umozurike, *The African Charter on Human and Peoples' Rights* (The Hague/Boston/London, Martinus Nijhoff Publishers, 1997), 240 p.

[27] Additional Protocol to the American Convention on Human Rights in the Area of Economic, Social and Cultural Rights, 'Protocol of San Salvador' O.A.S. Treaty Series No. 69

Rights. The Protocol of San Salvador is largely similar to the American Convention on Human Rights in defining State obligations. Article 1, which incorporates many of the elements of the nature of State obligations in Article 4 of the CRC and Article 2 (1) of the CESCR, states:

> 'The States Parties to this Additional Protocol to the American Convention on Human Rights undertake to adopt the necessary measures, both domestically and through international co-operation, especially economic and technical, to the extent allowed by their available resources, and taking into account their degree of development, for the purpose of achieving progressively and pursuant to their internal legislations, the full observance of the rights recognized in this Protocol.'

33. It is curious that the Article does not require that States should use the maximum extent of their available resources, but rather that they under-take to adopt measures 'to the extent allowed by their available resources'. Unfortunately, there is no jurisprudence to date from either the Inter-American Commission on Human Rights or the Inter-American Court to clarify whether this makes a significant difference from international stan-dards, and has the potential to lower the standard so that States need only to demonstrate that they have used the extent allowed by their available resources rather than maximum available resources. Further, there is a new element that appears in this Protocol, which does not appear in any other international or regional treaty when it requires States to take measures while also 'taking into account their degree of development.' However, the Inter-American Commission on Human Rights has stressed that Member States 'should take *all measures* necessary to ensure that the observance of economic, social and cultural rights does not diminish in any aspect over time.' The Commission has detailed a number of measures that States Parties should undertake, including that, regardless of the level of economic devel-opment, to guarantee a minimum threshold of economic, social and cultural rights, to guarantee social and economic data collection, to guarantee an economic environment that will enable the poor to participate in the polit-ical and economic decision-making process, and to ensure that socially disadvantaged groups, particularly minorities, do not suffer disproportionately from economic adjustment measures. It is therefore argued that the guidance developed by the Commission throughout the years points out that the there is in fact a duty on States to take steps to the maximum extent of

(1988), entered into force November 16, 1999, reprinted in *Basic Documents Pertaining to Human Rights in the Inter-American System*, OEA/Ser.L.V/II.82 doc.6 rev.1, 1992, 67.

their available resources, and that the level of development of the State should not be taken as an excuse for non-implementation of its obligations regarding economic, social and cultural rights.[28]

34. The *European Social Charter*[29] complements the European Convention on Human Rights and Fundamental Freedoms, in the field of economic and social rights. It sets out a number of rights and freedoms, but the main two articles in the Charter that deal with children directly are Articles 7 (the right of children and young persons to protection) and 17 (the right of children and young persons to social, legal and economic protection). However, other general articles in the Charter, including rights relating to housing, health, education, employment, social protection, movement of persons and non-discrimination, are obviously applicable to children.[30] The Charter does not include a specific article that sets out the nature of State obligations.

35. Given that the collective complaints mechanism of the Charter is only a few years old, there are as yet few opinions by the European Committee of Social Rights that relate to children.[31] However, in its very first case, concerning child labour, the Committee stated in relation to Article 7 that it 'acknowledges firstly the legal obligation assumed by the Government in accepting all of the European Social Charter and, more particularly, all of the paragraphs of Article 7, as well as in ratifying the Protocol providing for a system of collective complaints. It observes that to date, few States have accepted as many international commitments under the Charter.'[32] The Committee adds that it 'recalls that the aim and purpose of the Charter, being a human rights protection instrument, is to protect rights not merely theoretically, but also in fact. In this regard, it considers that the satisfactory application of Article 7 cannot be ensured solely by the operation of legislation if this is not effectively applied and rigorously supervised (see for example Conclusions XIII–3, pp. 283 and 286).'[33] It can be understood from this that the Committee believes that legislative and other measures should be adopted

---

[28] See further T. Melish, *o.c.* (note 17), pp. 53–63.

[29] European Social Charter, 529 U.N.T.S. 89, entered into force on 26 February 1965.

[30] The Charter was revised in 1996 adding new provisions.

[31] It guarantees a wide range of rights. Individuals cannot apply to the European Court of Human Rights for violation of the European Social Charter, as the Court supervises the application of the European Convention on Human Rights by the Member States of the Council of Europe, while complaints of violations of the Charter may be lodged with the European Committee of Social Rights.

[32] European Committee of Social Rights, *ICJ* v. *Portugal*, 12 October 1998, Complaint No. 1/ 1998, para. 23

[33] *Ibid.*, para. 25.

in order to implement obligations under the Charter. However, it is not clear from this what other measures need to be adopted.

36. As stated earlier, Article 1 (1) of the *African Charter on the Rights and Welfare of the Child* defines the nature of State obligations by requiring States Parties to take necessary steps, in accordance with their constitutional processes to adopt legislative measures. This Article adopts a similar formula to the CRC in relation to legislative and other measures, but does not include a specific provision related to the nature of State obligations regarding economic, social and cultural rights. The African Commission on Human and Peoples' Rights, has stated in an important decision concerning the pollution of the water and environment in Ogoniland of Nigeria due to activities by oil companies, and the responsibilities and duties of the government in this regard:

> 'It would be proper to establish what is generally expected of governments under the Charter and more specifically vis-à-vis the rights themselves. Internationally accepted ideas of the various obligations engendered by human rights indicate that all rights – both civil and political rights and social and economic rights – generate at least four levels of duties for a State that undertakes to adhere to a rights regime, namely the duty to *respect, protect, promote, and fulfil these rights.* These obligations universally apply to all rights and entail a combination of negative and positive duties. As a human rights instrument, the African Charter is not alien to these concepts.'[34]

37. This elaboration is similar to the interpretation of the CESCR and will be discussed separately below in the section on implementation. The Commission adds that 'governments have a duty to protect their citizens, not only through appropriate legislation and effective enforcement, but also by protecting them from damaging acts that may be perpetrated by private parties'[35] It is noticeable that the wording of Article 1 of the African Charter does not directly include language relating to 'maximum available resources' or 'progressive realization of the rights' as in the CRC and the CESCR. However, the Commission itself emphasizes in several of its decisions that the fulfilment of obligations concerning economic and social rights is largely dependent upon the presence of resources.[36]

---

[34] African Commission on Human Rights, *The Social and Economic Rights Action Centre and the Centre for Economic and Social Rights* v. *Nigeria*, 27 May 2002, ACHPR/COMM/A044/1, paras. 43–44.

[35] *Ibid.*, para. 57.

[36] For a more thorough analysis of the work of the African Commission on Human and People's Rights in the field of economic, social and cultural rights, see K. Olaniyan, *Nigeria, spoliation and International Human Rights*, (unpublished manuscript) (on file with the author), pp. 139–153.

CHAPTER THREE

SCOPE OF ARTICLE 4 OF THE CRC

1. *General Overview*

38. This chapter explores the different elements of Article 4 as identified earlier. The CRC is first compared to the CCPR and the CESCR. A brief overview of the drafting history of Article 4 is presented, followed by a short description of the reporting guidelines by the CRC Committee in relation to the provision. Specific elements of the reporting guidelines are referred to in the relevant sections throughout the document. A general overview elaborates on some elements of a general nature to Article 4. This is then followed by a discussion regarding legislative and other measures, resources, international co-operation and foreign debt, reservations and limitations on rights. Finally, there is a brief section on monitoring implementation.

1.1   *The CRC and the Two Covenants*

39. The two International Covenants on Civil and Political Rights and Economic, Social and Cultural Rights and their interpretation help to understand the nature of States Parties' obligations under the CRC. It is therefore important to understand the links between the three instruments. During the drafting of the CRC, one of the main questions raised was whether it should include rights that were already in the two Covenants. On the one hand, it was argued that if the Covenant rights were not included also in the CRC, this could undermine the applicability of these rights to children including, for example, certain civil and political rights such as freedom of expression, thought, conscience and religion and freedom of association. On the other hand, it was argued that by including in the CRC rights that were already enshrined in the Covenants, there was a risk of lowering the standards in the existing instruments which were already applicable to children. It was therefore decided that the CRC should consist of up to date and concrete provisions, and that it should be supplementary to already existing international treaties.[37]

---

[37] S. Detrick, *o.c.* (note 6), p. 16.

40. The uniqueness of the CRC, therefore, is that not only does it combine both sets of rights in one instrument but adds new ones. Further, many of the rights in the CRC cannot be identified simply as only civil, political, economic, social or cultural, but instead encapsulate different aspects of both sets of rights thereby reflecting their indivisibility.[38] By including in the CRC rights that were already in the Covenants, the drafters could change the language to accommodate the need for a slightly different approach in relation to children. For example, the CRC adds that, in relation to the child's freedom of thought, conscience, and religion, 'States Parties shall respect the rights and duties of the parents and, when applicable, legal guardians, to provide direction to the child in the exercise of his or her right in a manner consistent with the evolving capacities of the child.' (Article 14 (2)). Further, related to freedom of expression and also in order to ensure that the best interests of the child are respected at all times, the CRC provides that there should be guarantees that 'a child who is capable of forming his or her own views [should have] the right to express those views freely in all matters affecting the child' (Article 12 (1)).

41. A question that needs to be addressed at the outset is which are the economic, social and cultural rights, and which are the civil and political rights in the CRC? One approach could be to state that they are the same rights that can also be found in either of the Covenants. Another approach is to consider those which include language similar to that found in Article 4 regarding resources, as there are some provisions in the CRC that put the obligation on the state to realize the right, with a particular reference to progressive realization, or availability of resources, for example in relation to the survival and development of the child, and identify those as economic, social or cultural rights. A third approach would be to look at how the CRC Committee has grouped these rights in its reporting guidelines. In this regard, one difficulty has been the fact that the Committee has not always grouped rights in terms that are clearly associated with one or the other set of rights. For example, the Committee's guidelines include the heading 'Family environment and alternative care', which covers several provisions of the CRC including those related to family reunification, adoption, illicit transfer and non-return, as well as periodic figures on children placed on protective care or custody. Additionally, economic exploitation of children is included under 'Special Protection Measures' together with many other

---

[38] See further examples below.

forms of exploitation, including children in conflict with the law, armed conflict, refugee children, and sexual exploitation. It therefore combines areas that are traditionally classified as economic, together with those pertaining to civil rights. By not classifying the provisions under one set of rights or another, it seems that the CRC Committee wanted to review the CRC articles in terms of how rights inter-link with each other and their impact on the child's life.

42. However, can all the rights in the CRC be easily categorized as civil and political on one hand, or economic, social and cultural on the other? The right of parents or other legally responsible persons for the child to provide appropriate direction and guidance to the child (Article 5) can not be classified under one set of rights or another. There are also rights in the CRC that are not included in either of the Covenants, for example the right to rest and leisure (Article 31), the right to be protected against abduction and sale (Article 35), the right to protection from all forms of exploitation (Article 36) and the right to integration and social recovery (Article 39). Rather than being related to one particular category of rights, they are inextricably linked to a child's welfare, mental and psychological growth and development, together with the need for protection to ensure that the child lives a normal life where he or she goes to school, enjoys childhood, and develops naturally without any negative influences. These are therefore linked to several aspects of civil, or economic, or social or cultural rights reflecting their indivisibility and ensuring 'to the maximum extent possible the survival and development of the child' (Article 6 (2)).

43. This is reinforced by the CRC Committee stating that 'there is no simple or authoritative division, of human rights in general or of the Convention rights, into the two categories.'[39] It draws attention to the fact, that according to its reporting guidelines, it groups Articles 7 (registration at birth), 8 (preservation of identity), 13 to 17 (freedoms of expression, thought, conscience or religion, association, right to privacy, and importance of the mass media) and 37 (a) (freedom from torture) under the heading 'Civil rights and freedoms', but that many other articles in the CRC include elements of civil and political rights, e.g. Articles 2 (freedom from discrimination), 3 (best interests of the child), 6 (right to life) and 12 (right to express his/

---

[39] CRC Committee, *General Comment No. 5 on General Measures of Implementation of the Convention on the Rights of the Child* (UN Doc. CRC/GC/2003/5, 2003) (hereinafter: CRC Committee, General Comment No. 5), para. 6.

her views freely in matters affecting him/her). The Committee concludes that this reflects the inter-dependence and indivisibility of all human rights, that 'enjoyment of economic, social and cultural rights is inextricably intertwined with enjoyment of civil and political rights,' and that both sets of rights are justiciable.[40]

44. One should also note the difficulty in measuring human rights violations and the threshold beyond which they are said to have occurred. Obligations concerning civil and political rights according to the CCPR and the CRC are immediate. However, not enough attention has been given to studying in more depth what constitutes a violation of a child's right. This is amply demonstrated by the different approach required in the case of torture or cruel, inhuman or degrading treatment. For example, whilst flogging an adult ten times could, for example, constitute cruel treatment, it is hard to argue that this would not amount to torture in the case of a 7-year-old child.[41]

45. The difficulty also arises in measuring violations of economic, social and cultural rights, partly because of the progressive nature of these rights and partly in deciding the minimum core content below which conditions should not be allowed to fall, and therefore deciding the threshold for violations. However, several proposals have been made to measure these rights, most notably the Limburg Principles on the Implementation of the CESCR.[42]

1.2   The Drafting History of Article 4 of the CRC

46. The drafting history of the CRC helps to explain how and why the particular formula of Article 4 came about, including in relation to both

---

[40] *Ibid.*

[41] For the approach of the European Court of Human Rights in this area see ECtHR, *Costello-Roberts* v. *United Kingdom*, 25 March 1993, *Publications of the Court*, A247-C.

[42] Principle 72 provides that a State Party will be in violation of the Covenant (or the economic, social and cultural rights guaranteed under the CRC for this purpose), *inter alia*, if:
   '- it fails to take a step which it is required to take by the Covenant;
   - it fails to remove promptly obstacles which it is under a duty to remove to permit the immediate fulfillment of a right;
   - it fails to implement without delay a right which it is required by the Covenant to provide immediately;
   - it willfully fails to meet a generally accepted international minimum standard of achievement, which is within its powers to meet;
   - it applies a limitation to a right recognized in the Covenant other than in accordance with the Covenant;
   - it deliberately retards or halts the progressive realization of a right, unless it is acting within a limitation permitted by the Covenant or it does so due to a lack of available resources or force majeure;
   - it fails to submit reports as required under the Covenant.'

economic, social and cultural rights, and international co-operation.[43] The initial draft of the CRC presented by Poland did not contain an article similar to the current Article 4 of the CRC. However, observations and proposals by states pointed out the need to include a provision that is largely similar to Article 2 (1) of the CESCR.[44]

47. The open-ended working group established in 1979 to consider the question of a draft Convention on the Rights of the Child looked at a revised proposed provision by Poland concerning the nature of States Parties' obligations which stated: 'The States Parties to the Present Convention shall undertake appropriate measures individually and within the framework of international co-operation, particularly in the areas of economy, health and education for the implementation of the rights recognized in this Convention.'[45]

48. This was meant to apply to the implementation of all the rights in the Convention and not only economic, social and cultural rights. After several amendments and proposals were made, a new one was submitted which introduced for the first time the concept of 'in accordance with their available resources', but without specifying that this applies only to economic, social and cultural rights. It stated:

> 'The States Parties to the Present Convention shall undertake all appropriate administrative and legislative measures, in accordance with their available resources and, where needed, within the framework of international co-operation, for the implementation of the rights recognized in this Convention.'[46]

49. This became the Article adopted by the working group. The UN Secretary-General requested that a technical review of the draft be undertaken by the United Nations Secretariat, partly in order to compare the standards established by the Convention to those 'in other widely accepted human rights instruments'. The Secretary-General also requested comments from a number of specialized agencies and UN bodies, as well as the International Committee of the Red Cross (ICRC).[47]

---

[43] For a full background on the drafting of Article 4 of the CRC, see *Legislative History of the Convention of the Rights of the Child (1978-1989), Article 4 (Implementation of Rights)*, contained in UN Doc. HR/1995/Ser.1/article.4. This is a compilation of all relevant official documents of the drafting history of the Convention on the Rights of the Child, as prepared by the UN Centre for Human Rights.

[44] *Ibid.*, pp. 3–4.

[45] *Ibid.*, p. 5. This is taken from Commission on Human Rights Document E/CN.4/1349, 1979.

[46] *Ibid.*, p. 7. Also contained in paragraph 289 of the Commission on Human Rights Document E/CN.4/1475, 1981.

[47] *Ibid.*, p. 9. The views received are compiled in the *Technical review of the draft Convention on the Rights of the Child* (UN Doc. E/CN.4/1989/WG.1/CRP.1 and Add.1), 1989.

50. A very important comment received from UNICEF shifted the discussion around Article 4 (which at this stage was Article 5).[48] UNICEF drew attention to what it saw as the three main elements of the Article. These are 1) the obligation to implement, 2) 'in accordance with their available resources', and 3) 'where needed within the framework of international co-operation.' In relation to the first, UNICEF raised the question whether the inclusion of 'legislative and administrative measures' could be inclusive of all the 'appropriate' measures that could be adopted. Therefore, the organisation suggested that this should be amended to read 'all appropriate administrative, legislative, and other measures' in order to ensure that the text is inclusive of any measures that could and should be adopted.

51. In relation to the phrasing 'in accordance with their available resources', UNICEF drew attention for the first time to the fact that none of the obligations under the CCPR, CEDAW and CERD are subject to the availability of resources.[49] The organisation objected clearly and strongly stating that:

> 'Article 5 of the draft Convention would achieve a radical diminution of the standards contained in existing instruments and would run counter to all the assumptions that have hitherto governed the recognition of civil and political rights.'[50]

52. UNICEF then suggested the total deletion of the phrase 'in accordance with their available resources' from the Article. In relation to 'international co-operation', UNICEF stated that this recalled the pledge in Articles 55 and 56 of the UN Charter and that Article 2 (1) of the CESCR includes international assistance and co-operation, but added that it can be assumed that 'international co-operation' encompasses the notion of assistance. UNICEF concluded that there is no inconsistency between this phrasing and existing standards.[51]

53. This was therefore the first time during the drafting of the CRC that the notion of a different approach to the implementation of economic, social and cultural rights on one hand and civil and political rights on the other in relation to resources was raised. Several delegations consequently expressed concern that civil and political rights in the CCPR were not subject to the

---

[48] *Ibid.*, p. 9. The views of UNICEF are included in UN Doc. E/CN.4/1989/WG.1/CRP.1, pp. 17-20.
[49] *Ibid.*, p. 11.
[50] *Ibid.*
[51] *Ibid.*, p. 12.

availability of resources proviso, and should not be weakened by the CRC. They supported UNICEF's proposal for the deletion of the reference to availability of resources. Others, however, were against deletion, raising the economic difficulties faced by developing countries as justification for maintaining it.[52]

54. The several proposals that were then made to try to reach a compromise concluded that economic, social and cultural rights should be separated in a sentence that stated 'in accordance with their available resources with respect to economic, social and cultural rights.'[53] The final text that was proposed by the drafting group was identical to the current text of Article 4 and this was adopted unanimously.

1.3   Reporting Guidelines[54]

55. It is important to examine reporting guidelines as they shed more light on the interpretation of Article 4. The CRC Committee has issued guidelines regarding the form and content of initial and periodic reports relating to implementation of the Convention. Under the heading 'General Measures of Implementation', the CRC Committee groups Articles 4 together with Article 42 (to make the principles and provisions of the Convention widely known), and Article 44 (6) (to make States Parties' reports widely available to the public at large). Concerning Article 4, the Committee requests States Parties to provide information in initial reports on:[55]

'(a) The measures taken to harmonize national law and policy with provisions of the Convention; and
(b) Existing or planned mechanisms at national or local level for coordinating policies relating to children and for monitoring the implementation of the Convention.'

56. The General Guidelines for periodic reports regarding Article 4 require States Parties to report on measures adopted by the State including the

---

[52] *Ibid.*, p. 14.
[53] *Ibid.*, p. 13.
[54] Article 44 (1) of the CRC provides that States Parties undertake to submit to the Committee reports on the measures they have adopted which give effect to the rights recognized in the CRC and on the progress made in the enjoyment of those rights. Initial reports have to be submitted within two years of the entry into force of the Convention for the State Party concerned, and then every five years.
[55] CRC Committee, *General Guidelines Regarding the Form and Content of Initial Reports to be Submitted under Article 44, Paragraph 1 (b) of the Convention on the Rights of the Child*, (UN Doc. CRC/C/5, 1991), para. 9.

conclusion of bilateral and multilateral agreements in the field of children's rights, changes in legislation and practice, mechanisms and structures to coordinate and monitor the implementation of the CRC, policies and programs developed to implement the CRC, factors and difficulties faced, and plans envisaged to improve further children's rights. The periodic reports should also include information on follow-up to the CRC Committee's recommendations on the previous reports including measures taken to follow up on each recommendation and difficulties faced.[56] The Committee then discusses specific detailed questions regarding the different elements of Article 4. These will be discussed separately under each of the relevant headings below.

1.4   The Link Between Article 4 and Other Articles of the CRC

57. As stated earlier, according to the reporting guidelines, Article 4 is grouped with Articles 42 and 44 (6) under the heading 'General Measures of Implementation'.[57] Further, as Article 4 deals with the nature of State obligations, it relates naturally to all the substantive articles of the CRC.

58. Through its concluding observations, the CRC Committee has asked governments to pay particular attention to the full implementation of Article 4 in light of the general principles of the CRC. These are Article 2 (non-discrimination)), Article 3 (best interests of the child) and Article 6 (right to life, survival and development).[58] In addition, the CRC Committee has made a link between Article 4 and Article 12 (the child's right to express his or her views).[59] This link is emphasized in the reporting guidelines and General Comment No. 5.[60]

59. Further, language used in Article 4 is similar to that used in other articles of the CRC relating to 'maximum available resources' and to the notion of 'progressive realization'. For example, Article 6 requires States to 'ensure to the maximum extent possible the survival and development of the child'; Article 24 (1) includes the phrase 'the highest attainable standard of health'; and article 28 (1) regarding education includes 'achieving this right

---

[56] CRC Committee, *General Guidelines Regarding the Form and Content of Periodic Reports* (UN Doc. CRC/C/58, 1996), paras. 5 and 6.
[57] CRC Committee, *General Guidelines Regarding the Form and Content of Initial Reports, o.c.* (note 55).
[58] See CRC Committee, *General Comment No. 5, o.c.* (note 39), paras. 3 and 12.
[59] *Ibid.*, para. 12.
[60] *Ibid.*

progressively.' Article 23 asks States to encourage and ensure assistance to the disabled child 'subject to the available resources.' Article 27 concerning the right to an adequate standard of living requires States to assist parents and others responsible for the child to implement this right 'in accordance with national conditions and within their means.' This emphasizes the progressive nature of implementation of some of the rights enshrined in the CRC.

60. Language in Article 4 regarding international co-operation is also repeated in other articles of the CRC, albeit in slightly different formulation. For example, Article 24 (4) regarding right to health requires States 'to promote and encourage international co-operation with a view to achieving progressively the full realization of the right recognized in the present Article. In this regard, particular account shall be taken of the needs of developing countries.' Article 28 (3) places an obligation on States to 'promote and encourage international co-operation in matters relating to education', and Article 23 (4) emphasizes the need for exchange of information and knowledge in the field of preventive health care.

2. Legislative Measures

61. In the reporting guidelines for periodic reports, the CRC Committee asks in relation to Article 4 for information on measures adopted to bring national legislation and practice in full conformity with the principles and provisions of the Convention. This includes information on any comprehensive review of domestic legislation and any new laws or codes adopted.[61] The Committee further asks specifically about clarification on the status of the CRC in domestic law, including its recognition in the constitution or other legislation, the possibility of invoking provisions of the CRC in national courts, and its status in the event of a conflict with national legislation.[62] Some of these aspects are developed further through evidence from CRC Committee's conclusions and recommendations.

2.1 Status of the CRC in National Legal Systems

62. The Committee has asked States to clarify 'where [the] principle of 'self-execution' is applicable, and the precise meaning of statements indicating

---

[61] CRC Committee, *General Guidelines Regarding the Form and Content of Periodic Reports*, o.c. (note 56), para. 12.

[62] *Ibid.*, para. 13.

that the Convention 'has constitutional status' or 'has been incorporated' in the national legal order.'[63] The Committee stated that measures giving legal effect to the CRC within the domestic legal system should be considered fundamental. These measures could include 'effective remedies for the children, their parents and other relevant individuals or groups.'[64]

63. Further, incorporation of the CRC in the legislation should mean that the provisions of the Convention can be directly invoked before the courts and applied by national authorities. The CRC Committee is of the view that, in the event of a conflict between the CRC and national legislation or practice, the Convention should prevail.[65] This is based on Article 27 of the Vienna Convention on the Law of Treaties, which states: 'A Party may not invoke the provisions of its internal law as justification for its failure to perform a treaty.' Further, the CRC Committee adds that it is not sufficient to merely guarantee rights of the child in the constitution, even through specific provisions, but that specific legislation will need to be introduced.[66] The Committee also has specifically commended situations in which the Convention clearly takes precedence over domestic law where the two conflict.[67]

2.2   Review and Amendment of Legislation

64. The obligation to carry out legislative measures requires that there should be a comprehensive review of the legislation applicable to children to ensure that they are consistent with the obligations under the CRC. The CRC Committee stated that such review 'needs to consider the Convention not only article by article, but also holistically, recognizing the interdependence and indivisibility of human rights.'[68] The Committee emphasizes that needs to be continuous of all existing legislation, and all new proposed legislation should be reviewed from a child-rights approach.[69]

65. In its concluding observations, the CRC Committee has recommended that laws and administrative regulations related to children should be reviewed to ensure that they are rights-based and conform to international

---

[63] 10th Anniversary Commemorative Meeting (UN Doc. CRC/C/87, 1999), Annex IV, para. 291 (d).
[64] *Ibid.*
[65] CRC Committee, *General Comment No. 5, o.c.* (note 39), para. 20.
[66] *Ibid.,* para. 21.
[67] R. Hodgkin and P. Newell, *o.c.* (note 1), p. 66.
[68] CRC Committee, *General Comment No. 5, o.c.* (note 39), para. 18.
[69] *Ibid.*

human rights standards, including the CRC, ensure speedy promulgation of any needed amendments, and that adequate provision is made for their effective implementation.[70] Allocation of resources is therefore essential not only to deliver services, but also for promulgation and implementation of legislation, policies and regulations. Concerned about the frequent lack of clarity in legislation, the CRC Committee has also stated that laws should be based on a child's rights approach, be sufficiently clear and precise, published, and accessible to the public.[71]

66. The Committee was clearly concerned when provisions related to children were scattered throughout domestic law.[72] On some occasions, the Committee has called on States to consider adopting a comprehensive single law or code for children, embodying the provisions and principles of the CRC, and providing a legal foundation at the domestic level for its implementation.[73] However, in its General Comment No. 5, the CRC Committee took a slightly different approach, and while welcoming the development by States of consolidated children's rights statutes, reminded them of the need to ensure 'that all relevant 'sectoral' laws (on education, health, justice and so on) reflect consistently the principles and standards of the Convention.'[74]

2.3   Customary or Religious Laws

67. The Committee has also made particular reference to customary law, where that law is applied, and recommended that steps should be taken to harmonize this with the CRC.[75] The Committee also asked that interpretation of religious laws should be reconciled with fundamental human rights.[76] For example, '[n]oting the universal values of equality and tolerance inherent in Islam, the Committee observes that narrow interpretations of Islamic texts by State authorities are impeding the enjoyment of many human rights

---

[70] See for example the following concluding observations of the CRC Committee: Belgium (UN Doc. CRC/C/15/Add.178, 2002) para. 9; Burkina Faso (UN Doc CRC/C/15/Add.19, 1994), para. 15; and Algeria (UN Doc. CRC/C/15/Add.76, 1997), paras. 12 and 29.

[71] CRC Committee, *Concluding Observations*: Libya (UN Doc. CRC/C/15/Add.209, 2000) para. 8 (c).

[72] See for example CRC Committee, *Concluding Observations*: Lao People's Democratic Republic (CRC/C/15/Add.78, 1997).

[73] See for example: CRC Committee, *Concluding Observations*: Libya, *o.c.* (note 71), para. 8 (a); Burkina Faso (UN Doc. CRC/C/15/Add.193, 2002) para. 8 (b).

[74] CRC Committee, *General Comment No. 5*, *o.c.* (note 39), para. 22.

[75] *Ibid.*, para. 8 (a).

[76] CRC Committee, *Concluding Observations*: Libya, *o.c.* (Note 71), para. 8 (b). The reference here is to the Islamic Shari'a laws.

protected under the Convention.'[77] It should be noted in this context that several UN special rapporteurs and treaty bodies have expressed concern over the use of religious law as an excuse by States to not implement their obligations according to international standards.[78]

2.4   *Legislative Measures for All Rights*

68. Legislative and administrative measures are not related only to civil and political rights, but rather to all the principles and rights enshrined in the CRC. For example, whilst laws are needed to prohibit torture and to ensure proper protection when children come into conflict with the law, at the same time, legislation is also needed to protect children's right to education, and from exploitation in the labour market. In this regard, the CRC Committee 'emphasizes that economic, social and cultural rights, as well as civil and political rights, must be regarded as justiciable. It is essential that domestic law sets out entitlements in sufficient detail to enable remedies for non-compliance to be effective.'[79] The CESCR Committee states that 'in many instances, legislation is highly desirable and in some cases [it] may even be indispensable. For example, it may be difficult to combat discrimination effectively in the absence of a sound legislative foundation for the necessary measures. In fields such as health, the protection of children and mothers, and education . . . legislation may also be an indispensable element for many purposes.'[80] This reaffirms the importance of legislation for the enjoyment of social, economic and cultural rights.

---

[77] CRC Committee, *Concluding Observations:* Saudi Arabia (UN Doc. CRC/C/15/Add.148, 2001), para. 6.

[78] For example, the Special Rapporteur on Torture in relation to corporal punishment said 'the Government's invocation of judicial independence in the application of Shari'a . . . does not relieve the State . . . from its obligation under international law to prevent the infliction of cruel, inhuman and degrading punishment.' The Special Rapporteur, highlighting a very important aspect of this debate, went on to note the fact that there exists a great divergence of views among Islamic scholars and clerics concerning the obligations of States in relation to corporal punishment and that the overwhelming majority of Member States of the Organization of the Islamic Conference do not implement corporal punishment in their domestic laws. *Report of the UN Special Rapporteur on Torture to the Commission on Human Rights* (UN Doc. E/CN.4/1997/7, 10 January 1997), para. 10. In the case of Bahrain, the CRC Committee expressed concern that 'Shari'a remains uncodifed and is applied in its classical sense without reference to State legislation; and because it is uncodified the system may be subject to arbitrariness, inconsistencies, and lack of uniformity between judgements between different qadis, or judges; between Shi'a and Sunni departments; and disparities with decisions of the secular courts.' CRC Committee, *Concluding Observations:* Bahrain (UN Doc. CRC/C/15/Add.175), para. 5.

[79] CRC Committee, *General Comment No. 5, o.c.* (note 39), para. 25.

[80] CESCR Committee, *General Comment No. 3 on the Nature of States Parties' Obligations* (contained in UN Doc. HRI/GEN/1/Rev.7, 1990), para. 3.

2.5 *Immediate Obligations*

69. The obligation to take legislative measures according to Article 4 of the CRC is an immediate obligation. As discussed earlier, the wording of Article 4 of the CRC is largely similar to that of Article 2 of the CCPR and Article 2 (1) of the CESCR. The two treaty bodies responsible for monitoring the implementation of the two Covenants have issued general comments regarding the nature of States Parties' obligations. The CRC Committee stated that 'in international human rights law, there are articles similar to Article 4 of the Convention, setting out overall implementation obligations, such as Article 2 of the CCPR and Article 2 of the CESCR. The Human Rights Committee and the Committee on Economic, Social and Cultural Rights have issued general comments in relation to these provisions which should be seen as complementary to the present general comment and which are referred to below.'[81]

70. The Human Rights Committee stated that '[t]he requirement under Article 2, paragraph 2, to take steps to give effect to the Covenant rights is unqualified and of immediate effect. A failure to comply with this obligation cannot be justified by reference to political, social, cultural or economic considerations within the State.'[82] Similarly, the CESCR Committee has stated that, while obligations related to economic, social and cultural rights contained in the Covenant are generally progressive, there are also obligations of immediate effect, for example, 'to take steps' to ensure and to guarantee the rights without discrimination.'[83] These comments clearly demonstrate that obligations under the CRC are immediate, not only in relation to civil and political rights, but also in the context of economic, social and cultural rights.

3. *Resource Allocation and Progressive Realization*

71. The wording of the CRC differs from Article 2 (1) of the CESCR in that the former does not mention 'progressive realization' while the latter does. However, the CRC Committee has stressed that, despite this explicit omission, the CRC does implicitly introduce the concept of 'progressive realization'

---

[81] CRC Committee, *General Comment No. 5, o.c.* (note 39), para. 5.
[82] Human Rights Committee, *General Comment No. 31 on the Nature of the General Legal Obligation Imposed on States Parties to the Covenant* (CCPR/C/74/CRP.4/Rev.6), para. 14.
[83] CESCR Committee, *General Comment No. 3 on the Nature of States Parties' Obligations, o.c.* (note 80), para. 1.

of rights,[84] and that, like the approach taken by the CESCR Committee, while the realization of economic, social and cultural rights is progressive, the obligation to take steps is an immediate one. Such steps should be taken within a reasonably short timeframe and 'should be deliberate, concrete and targeted as clearly as possible towards meeting the obligations.'[85]

72. The Inter-American Commission on Human Rights, in a consultative opinion, elaborated on the nature of States Parties' obligations in relation to progressive implementation, making specific reference to Article 4 of the CRC. The Commission stated that 'the full exercise of children's economic, social and cultural rights has been related to the possibilities of the bounded State (article 4 of the CRC), which must guarantee the highest effort, constant and deliberately, to assure children's access to these rights, and its enjoyment, avoiding retrocesses and unjustified delays', and assigning the maximum available resources to its fulfilment.[86]

73. The requirement that the State must guarantee 'highest effort', 'constant', and 'deliberate' echoes the words 'deliberate', 'concrete and 'targeted' of the CESCR Committee, and constitutes a useful indicator as to whether the State is doing all that it can 'to the maximum extent of its available resources' in relation to implementing the economic, social and cultural rights of children.

74. However, it remains unclear whether this means that allocations of resources for implementing the economic, social and cultural rights of children should be prioritized in terms of the overall budget allocated to children, or that the children's budget should be prioritized in relation to the overall national budget. The Committee has observed that 'the maximum extent of available resources' should prioritize children in resource allocation and that this should facilitate universal provision of basic but good quality social services for children.[87]

75. Further, it should be stressed that while the obligation to implement civil and political rights in the CRC is immediate, the realization of these rights is also dependent on the allocation of resources. By way of illustration, the Human Rights Committee states that measures to be adopted to protect

---

[84] CRC Committee, *General Comment No. 5, o.c.* (note 39), para. 7.

[85] CESCR Committee, *General Comment No. 3 on the Nature of States Parties' Obligations, o.c.* (note 80), para. 2.

[86] Inter-American Commission on Human Rights, *Consultative Opinion OC-17/2002 Concerning 'Juridical Condition and Human Rights of the Child'*, 27 August 2002, para. 81.

[87] CRC Committee, *10th Anniversary Commemorative Meeting* (UN Doc. CRC/C/87, 1999) Annex IV, para. 291 (o).

children's rights according to the CCPR 'may also be economic, social and cultural. For example, every possible economic and social measure should be taken to reduce infant mortality and to eradicate malnutrition among children and to prevent them from being subjected to acts of violence and cruel and inhuman treatment or from being exploited by means of forced labour or prostitution, or by their use in the illicit trafficking of narcotic drugs, or by any other means.'[88] These rights that the Human Rights Committee is concerned about are also enshrined in the CRC, and therefore the interpretation of the Committee in that regard is essential to understand obligations regarding civil and political rights in the CRC.

3.1 *Limited Resources*

76. A difficult question that poses itself is whether cuts can take place to budgets allocated to children during a period of economic recession. In such a situation, governments should identify priorities with respect to children's rights in order to ensure that funds are allocated 'to the maximum extent of available resources'. Even in such cases, the CRC Committee has expressed concern about resulting decreases in budgetary allocation for children, and asked that governments continue to prioritize allocations of funds to ensure the effective implementation of children's rights.[89]

77. In so doing, the CRC Committee concurs with the comment by the CESCR Committee that even where the available resources are inadequate, the obligation remains on a State Party to ensure the widest possible enjoyment of the relevant rights under the prevailing circumstances.[90] In this context, the CESCR Committee has stated that it is important to distinguish between the inability of a State Party to comply with its obligations compared to its unwillingness to do so. A State which is unwilling to use the maximum of its available resources for the realization of a certain right is in violation of its obligations towards the realization of that right.[91] On the other hand, if resource constraints render it impossible for a State Party to

---

[88] Human Rights Committee, *General Comment No. 17 on the Rights of the Child* (contained in UN Doc. HRI/GEN/1/Rev.7, 1989), para. 3

[89] See for example CRC Committee, *Concluding Observations*: Jamaica (UN Doc CRC/C/15/Add.210, 2003), paras. 17 and 18; Israel (UN Doc. CRC/C/15/Add.195, 2002), para. 19. In the case of Israel, the CRC Committee asked that the government continue to prioritize budgetary allocation for children belonging to the most vulnerable groups (e.g. Israeli Arab children, Bedouin children and children of foreign workers).

[90] *Ibid.*, at para. 8.

[91] See for example CESCR Committee, *General Comment No. 14 on the Right to the Highest Attainable Standard of Health* (contained in UN Doc. HRI/GEN/1/Rev.7, 2000), para. 47. The

comply fully with its obligations 'it [still] has the burden of justifying that every effort has nevertheless been made to use all available resources at its disposal in order to satisfy, as a matter of priority, the obligations outlined above.'[92]

3.2   Resource Allocations for Social Services

78. In its reporting guidelines for periodic reports, the CRC Committee asks for specific information on measures taken to ensure the implementation of economic, social and cultural rights of children to the maximum extent of available resources by using indicators or target figures to show what proportion of the budget is devoted to social expenditure on children, and measures taken to ensure that the disparities between different regions and groups of children are bridged.

79. The CRC Committee has made it repeatedly clear that resources encompass both human and financial means, and that therefore allocation should include ensuring that there are sufficient numbers of qualified professionals in the various sectors (*e.g.* health, education, social services) working with and for children. In practice, this requires allocation of enough funds to ensure that professional staff are adequately trained and have sufficient capacity to respond to priorities.[93]

3.3   Budgetary Analysis and Review

80. It is very important that the allocation of resources is subject to regular review and analysis of relevant data and indicators in order to determine whether adequate sums have been made available in order to achieve the necessary progress in the realization of rights. This analysis should identify clearly the amount and proportion spent on children segregated by race, gender, geographical area, etcetera.[94] The-CRC Committee has emphasized that 'sufficient and reliable data collection, disaggregated to enable identification of discrimination and/or disparities in the realization of rights, is an essential part of implementation.'[95]

---

concept distinguishing between 'unwillingness and inability' was used in subsequent general comments by the CESCR Committee.

[92] *Ibid.*

[93] See CRC Committee, *Concluding Observations*: Estonia (UN Doc. CRC/C/15/Add.196, 2003) para. 16 (d); Gabon (UN Doc. CRC/C/15/Add.171, 2002) para. 13 (b); Morocco (UN Doc. CRC/C/15/Add.211, 2004) para. 12 (a).

[94] CRC Committee, *General guidelines Regarding the Form and Content of Periodic Reports, o.c.* (note 56), para. 7.

[95] CRC Committee, *General Comment No. 5, o.c.* (note 39), para. 48.

81. On some occasions, the CRC Committee has expressed concern that there is either no integrated budget for children, or that the budget allocated to children is not sufficient, or not commensurate to the overall budget increase, and that it should be increased.[96] The Committee has also noted in some cases a decline in allocation of funds for children, even despite economic development, or that budgettary allocations to children are not commensurate with those of other States with a similar level of economic development.[97] Such cases clearly reflect the fact that some States are failing to implement their obligations under the CRC, not because of inability, but due to a lack of will and planning.

3.4 Disadvantaged Groups

82. The CRC Committee stresses that, within the general framework of prioritizing budgettary allocations for children, greatest attention should be given to those belonging to disadvantaged groups, even when resources are limited.[98]

83. In this context, policies for poverty reduction are essential to achieve the realization of rights for children, and to strengthen income redistribution policies in favour of families living in extreme poverty. It is clear that children who come from poor families or are themselves poor, that they are vulnerable to different forms of exploitation, including exploitative forms of child labour, child prostitution, and child soldiering. Special investment needs to be in place in order to ensure that those children do not slip into such situations. The Millennium Development Goals are of particular relevance here. The first goal, for example, is to eradicate extreme poverty and hunger by reducing by half the proportion of people who suffer from hunger by 2015.[99] The CRC Committee has also noted on several occasions the disparity in the implementation of the CRC between rural and urban areas, and that cases of low allocation of resources for children in rural areas may have had a disproportionate effect on them.[100]

---

[96] See CRC Committee, *Concluding Observations*: Chile (UN Doc. CRC/C/15/Add.173, 2002) para. 14; Burkina Faso (UN Doc. CRC/C/15/Add.193, 2002) para. 16 (a);

[97] See CRC Committee, *Concluding Observations*: Republic of Korea (UN Doc. CRC/C/15/Add.197, 2003) para. 19; Solomon Islands (UN Doc. CRC/C/15/Add.208, 2003) para. 13; Poland (UN Doc. CRC/C/15/Add.194,2002) para. 17; and Sri Lanka (UN Doc. CRC/C/15/Add.207, 2003) para. 17.

[98] CRC Committee, *General Comment No. 5, o.c.* (note 39), para. 8. See also CRC Committee, *Concluding Observations*: Cyprus (UN Doc. CRC/C/15/Add.205, 2003) para. 16; Eritrea (UN Doc. CRC/C/15/Add.204,2003) para. 13.

[99] See further on Millennium Development Goals (Section III.4.3 below).

[100] See for example CRC Committee, *Concluding Observations*: Romania (UN Doc. CRC/C/15/Add.199, 2003) para. 13; Spain (UN Doc. CRC/C/15/Add.185,2002) para. 18 (a).

3.5   Roles of Different Sectors

84. In addition to the public sector, human rights implementation is achieved through a combination of private and voluntary sector delivery. This arrangement has been acknowledged by the CRC Committee in its frequent requests to States Parties to 'identify the amount and proportion of the State budget spent on children in the public, private and NGO sectors in order to evaluate the impact and effect of the expenditure and also, in view of the costs, the accessibility and the quality and effectiveness of the services for children in the different sectors.'[101] At the same time, the Committee has urged governments not to devolve responsibility for the implementation of children's rights to NGOs without the necessary provision of resources.[102]

85. In an important case in Costa Rica concerning the role of the nongovernmental sector, the Supreme Court of Justice, sitting as a Constitutional Court, ruled against the Ministry of Economy and National Treasury for withholding funding from the sector and by so doing violating fundamental economic and social rights. The appellants, representing organizations providing social services, claimed that during the fiscal year 2000, they had not received the funds due to them pursuant to law No. 7972. The respondents countered that the Constitution empowered them to allocate public revenues according to the needs identified by them and that, had the funds been provided to the said organizations, a large number of areas essential to public well-being would have been left without funding. The Court considered that the organizations which ought to have received the revenues from the tax levied by Law No. 7972 made it possible for the State to comply with its obligations in respect of the rights to life, health, education, protection of minors, the elderly, the family, etcetera, and therefore, that the Executive Power's failure to draw the funds as required adversely affected the said fundamental rights or, at least, generated an imminent adverse effect upon them.[103]

---

[101] See for example CRC Committee, *Concluding Observations*: Andorra (UN Doc. CRC/C/15/Add.176, 2002) para. 17; Bahrain (UN Doc. CRC/C/15/Add.180, 2002) para. 14 (c); Cyprus (UN Doc. CRC/C/15/Add.205, 2003), para. 16; Gabon (UN Doc. CRC/C/15/Add.171, 2002), para. 13 (a); Kazakhstan (UN Doc. CRC/C/15/Add.213, 2003) para. 17 (c).

[102] CRC Committee, *Report on the twenty-first session* (UN Doc. CRC/C/87), Annex IV, para. 291 (v).

[103] *María Isabel Chamorro Santamaría, Guillermo Constenla Umaña, Luis Fishman Zonzinski and José Merino del Río v. the Minister of Treasury and the National Treasurer*, Costa Rica, the Supreme Court sitting as Constitutional Court.

3.6   Immediate and Progressive Implementation

86. Does the progressive nature of the implementation of economic, social and cultural rights mean that the implementation of civil, political and other rights in the CRC must be immediate, while the obligations in relation to economic, social and cultural rights are progressive? The very nature of implementation for all human rights is naturally progressive. The obligation to take steps is immediate. For example, whilst laws should be put in place immediately to prohibit torture, and measures taken immediately to achieve an end to the practice, the realization of complete cessation will naturally be progressive; or at least that is the reality in many countries, as it will depend on changes in legislation, training of prison guards and law enforcement officers, etcetera. The same applies to the full guarantee of fair trials, where the obligation is immediate to take steps to guarantee the right. However, actually ending unfair trials will take time, requiring changes in legislation, orders, and procedures, together with the training of law enforcement officials and judges, among other measures. This can apply to many other, if not all, civil and political rights.[104]

87. Measuring the progress in realizing economic, social and cultural rights poses clear problems. It does not only require an assessment of current programs and performance, but also a determination on whether a State is moving expeditiously towards the goal of full implementation, using the most extent of available resources. The development of jurisprudence on economic, social and cultural rights reflects, however, that progressive realization does not allow for retrogressiveness, stand-still, or indefinite postponement of implementation. Further, there are immediate obligations associated with progressive realization.

88. While the full realization of different relevant economic, social and cultural rights may be achieved progressively, steps towards that goal must be taken either before or within a reasonably short time after ratification.[105] The drafting history of the CESCR shows clearly that it was generally agreed that 'the notion of implementation at the earliest possible moment is implicit

---

[104] Human Rights Committee, *General Comment No. 17 on the Rights of the Child, o.c.* (note 88), para. 3.
[105] See for a further discussion on the nature of State obligations regarding economic, social and cultural rights, especially from the view of the drafting history of the ICESCR, P. Alston and G. Quinn, 'The Nature and Scope of States Parties' Obligations under the International Covenant on Economic, Social and Cultural Rights', *Human Rights Quarterly* 9, 1987, pp. 156–229.

in Article 2 [of the CESCR] as a whole'.[106] It is therefore clear that there is an immediate obligation related to economic, social and cultural rights. The CESCR Committee stated that 'any deliberate retrogressive measures . . . would require the most careful consideration and would need to be fully justified by reference to the totality of the [economic, social and cultural] rights provided . . . in the context of the full use of the maximum available resources.'[107] Immediate obligations include taking steps, and ensuring that relevant rights are exercised without discrimination. Many rights are capable of immediate application, including the duty to ensure protection of the family, or ensuring that primary education is compulsory, free and available for all.[108]

89. The Maastricht Guidelines clarify that in many cases, compliance with obligations related to economic, social and cultural rights may be undertaken by most States with relative ease and without significant resource implications.[109] State practice shows that, as this clearly implies 'essential cost-free measures can be undertaken by States that will result in the enjoyment of certain economic, social and cultural rights.'[110] Guideline 14 (e) of the Maastricht Guidelines states that the 'adoption of any deliberate retrogressive measure that reduces the extent to which any such right is guaranteed' is a violation of that right. The Guidelines further clarify that a State is in violation of its obligations regarding economic, social and cultural rights when it fails to remove promptly obstacles in order to permit the immediate fulfillment of a right, and the failure to implement without delay a right which a State is under the duty to provide.[111]

90. Progressive realization should not be interpreted to imply that a State is allowed to defer indefinitely its efforts to ensure full realization of the rights.[112] A violation of economic, social and cultural rights occurs when

---

[106] *Ibid.*, p. 172.

[107] CESCR Committee, *General Comment No. 3 on the Nature of States Parties' Obligations, o.c.* (note 80), para. 9. The CRC Committee stated that this General Comment should be regarded as complementary to the CRC Committee's General Comment No. 5. See CRC Committee, *General Comment No. 5, o.c.* (note 39), para. 5.

[108] CESCR Committee, *General Comment No. 3 on the Nature of States Parties' Obligations, o.c.* (note 80), paras. 1, 2 and 5.

[109] Maastricht Guidelines, Guideline 10.

[110] For a commentary on the Maastricht Guidelines, see V. Dankwa, C. Flinterman, and S. Leckie, 'Commentary to the Maastricht Guidelines on the Violations of Economic, Social and Cultural Rights', *Human Rights Quarterly* 20, 1998, pp. 705–730.

[111] Maastricht Guidelines 15 (g) and (h).

[112] Limburg Principles, Principle 21.

there is obstruction of or halt to progressive realization of rights, unless the State is acting within limitations permitted under the relevant treaties.[113]

91. In her ground breaking Article, Audrey Chapman suggests that 'the evaluation of the performance of States Parties has largely focussed on assessment of progressive realization rather than on identification of violations.'[114] This lead to the development of a violations approach to assessing progress of implementation of economic, social and cultural rights, which in turn lead to the Limburg Principles and the Maastricht Guidelines.[115]

4. International Co-operation and Foreign Debt

92. Article 4 requires that for the implementation of economic, social and cultural rights, States undertake such measures, where needed, 'within the framework of international co-operation.' The principle of international co-operation is reflected in the CRC and the CESCR as interpreted by the respective monitoring bodies.[116] The CRC Committee links the concept of international co-operation with progressive realization of rights. The Committee believes that 'States need to be able to demonstrate that they have implemented 'to the maximum extent of their available resources' and, where necessary, have sought international co-operation. The CRC Committee believes that when States ratify the Convention 'they take upon themselves obligations not only to implement it within their jurisdiction, but also to contribute, through international co-operation, to global implementation.'[117] Consequently, international co-operation for development and thus for the realization of economic, social and cultural rights is an obligation of all States. The CESCR Committee also believes that this is a particular duty for those States which are in a position to assist others.[118]

---

[113] Maastricht Guidelines, Guideline 14 (f).

[114] See A.R. Chapman, 'A "Violations Approach" for Monitoring the International Covenant on Economic, Social and Cultural Rights', *Human Rights Quarterly* 18, 1996, p. 30.

[115] See further paragraph 16 above.

[116] This is based on Articles 55 and 56 of the UN Charter, which require Member States of the UN to pledge themselves to take joint and separate action in co-operation with the UN, to achieve 'the creation of conditions of stability and well-being which are necessary for peaceful and friendly relations among nations based on respect for the principle of equal rights and self-determination of peoples.'

[117] *Ibid.*

[118] CESCR Committee, *General Comment No. 3 on the Nature of States Parties' Obligations, o.c.* (note 80), para. 14.

93. Several targets have been proposed for the delivery of assistance. For example, in 1970, the United Nations General Assembly set the international aid target at 0.7 per cent of the Gross National Product (GNP). In addition, the 20/20 initiative of the United Nations Development Program (UNDP) encourages donor countries to allocate at least 20 percent of foreign aid to human priority goals, such as primary education, primary health care, safe drinking water and sanitation, whilst, in turn, recipient countries must allocate 20 percent of public expenditure to enable universal access to basic social services.[119]

94. Translating international co-operation into reality has been achieved mainly through the elaboration of agreements, projects or programmes taking a variety of forms, including technical assistance from UN agencies, bodies and organs and bilateral and multilateral aid treaties of aid and loans. However, the resultant debt has frequently left poorer countries with large amounts to repay, sometimes so great that a considerable proportion of a country's GDP is solely used for repayment.

4.1   Children and International Aid

95. Debt can also have a particularly adverse affect on children as governments spend part of their available resources for repaying debt rather than for social policies and services in order to guarantee children's rights. In 2000, the UN General Assembly Special Session on Children (UNGASS) concluded as part of its final report titled 'A World Fit for Children' that '[c]hronic poverty remains the single biggest obstacle to meeting the needs, protecting and promoting the rights of children. It must be tackled on all fronts, from the provision of basic social services to the creation of employment opportunities, from the availability of microcredit to investment in infrastructure, and from debt relief to fair trade practices.'[120] The report points out the necessity of 'speedy and concerted action to address effectively the debt problems of the least developed countries, low-income developing countries and middle-income developing countries in a comprehensive, equitable, development-oriented and durable way through various national

---

[119] For a discussion of the 20/20 initiative and its impact on children see *Implementing the 20/20 Initiative*, (UNDP, UNESCO, UNFPA, UNICEF, WHO and the World Bank, UNICEF, 1998), 30 pp.

[120] *A World Fit for Children*, the outcome of the UN General Assembly Special Session on Children 8–10 October 2002, adopted by the General Assembly (UN Doc. A/RES/S-27/2, 2002); para. 18.

and international measures designed to make their debt sustainable in the long term and thereby to improve their capacity to deal with issues relating to children, including, as appropriate, existing orderly mechanisms for debt reduction such as debt swaps for projects aimed at meeting the needs of children.'[121] Several methods of debt relief have been practised since the mid 1990s including debt swaps, cancellation, rescheduling, and refinancing.

96. In its general guidelines for periodic reports, the CRC Committee has asked for information about measures taken to ensure that children, particularly those belonging to disadvantaged groups, are protected against the adverse effects of economic policies and the proportion of international aid at multilateral and bilateral level allocated to child focused programs. In respect of donor countries, the Committee has asked for information on the percentage of the national budget allocated to international co-operation, together with the percentage of that contribution allocated to health, education, social and other such sectors.[122]

97. While emphasizing the importance of seeking international assistance, the CRC Committee has also expressed some concern about the danger of being solely dependent on foreign assistance, in so far as it could jeopardize the sustainability of resources.[123] Consequently, it has recommended that governments establish clear policies for the allocation of resources for children, including those obtained through international agency and bilateral agreements.

98. Emphasizing that the concept of 'maximum available resources' includes those that are available both internally in the country and externally through international co-operation and assistance,[124] the CRC Committee has also recommended to donor countries to increase their allocation of resources to children. For example, in the case of Eritrea, the Committee was concerned that the funds allocated through the government and development assistance was not enough, and recommended that both the government

---

[121] *Ibid.*, para. 52 (c).
[122] CRC Committee, *General Guidelines Regarding the Form and Content of Periodic Reports, o.c.* (note 56), paras. 20 and 21.
[123] See for example CRC Committee, *Concluding Observations*: Guinea Bissau (UN Doc. CRC/C/15/Add.177) paras. 11 and 12.
[124] See also CESCR Committee, *General Comment No. 3 on the Nature of States Parties' Obligations, o.c.* (note 80), para. 13, where the CESCR Committee states that this interpretation was the intention of the drafters of the CESCR.

and international donors 'reopen their dialogue, in particular with regard to the implementation of children's rights.'[125]

99. The Committee has also noted on some occasions that, while overseas development assistance is increasing in absolute terms, it is not doing so relative to GDP. Hence, the encouragement to affected countries to strive to achieve the UN 0.7 per cent target of GDP.[126] Furthermore, the Committee has recommended that the principle of allocating the maximum extent of available resources should also be applied to activities carried out by donor countries through international development aid and co-operation.[127]

100. Finally, the CRC Committee has recommended that all UN agencies should be guided by the Convention and should mainstream children's rights throughout their activities, which naturally include technical assistance and co-operation.[128]

4.2   The World Bank and the IMF

101. While a thorough discussion of international co-operation, foreign debt, and financial policies is beyond the scope of this paper, a few important aspects are worth highlighting in relation to how they impact on the implementation of the CRC. The aid policies of international financial institutions, such as the World Bank and the International Monetary Fund (IMF), have been the subject of increasingly widespread criticism, particularly the Structural Adjustment Programs (SAPs), initiated in the 1970s. For example, Oxfam is of the opinion that 'IMF-inspired policies have continued to undermine the access of poor people to education, not just by cutting basic social-service budgets, but also by intensifying household poverty.'[129] The aid agency concludes that 'a major negative side effect has been an increase in poverty and unemployment. In fact, SAPs can contribute to the structural causes of poverty by advancing reforms that eliminate minimum

---

[125] CRC Committee, *Concluding Observations*: Eritrea (UN Doc. CRC/C/15/Add.204, 2003) para. 13.

[126] CRC Committee, *Concluding Observations*: Iceland (UN Doc. CRC/C/15/Add.203, 2003) paras. 16 and 17.

[127] See for example CRC Committee, *Concluding Observations*: Italy (UN Doc. CRC/C/15/Add.198, 2003) para. 9; United Kingdom (UN Doc. CRC/C/15/Add.188, 2002) para. 10.

[128] CRC Committee, *General Comment No. 5, o.c.* (note 39), para. 26.

[129] *International co-operation: the record since Jomtien*, in *Education Report*, p. 234, available on. http://www.oxfam.org.uk/what_you_can_do/campaign/educationnow/downloads/edreport/Chap%205.pdf.

wages, weaken environmental laws, reduce or eliminate social programs that help the poor, and promote rapid privatization of government enterprises, allowing the well-connected elite to profit from the monetary benefits.'[130]

102. The Commission on Human Rights' Independent Expert on the Effects on SAPs and Foreign Debt, noting that the adverse effects of such policies are widely acknowledged and well documented, has recommended to the Economic and Social Council and the General Assembly of the UN to 'call on Member States, [international financial institutions] and all other stakeholders to take every appropriate measure to redress and/or alleviate poverty and conditions that give rise to indebtedness and the adverse effects of measures adopted to comply with SAPs.'[131]

103. It is also well documented that children have been among the worst affected by SAPs, and this is reflected in the deliberations of the CRC Committee. The Committee, emphasising that since economic policies are never neutral in their effect on children's rights, has expressed its deep concern of the often negative effects on children of structural adjustment programmes and transition to a market economy and concluded that '[t]he implementation duties of Article 4 and other provisions of the Convention demand rigorous monitoring of the effects of such changes and adjustment of policies to protect children's economic, social and cultural rights.'[132] In the Committee's General Discussion Day on Economic Exploitation on Children in 1993, it, after inviting the World Bank and the IMF to a discussion about the need to protect the rights of the child in programs of economic reform, noted 'that groups of children in both poor and rich countries have been victimized by sweeping measures to curb inflation and encourage growth. Social allocations have been cut in drastic proportion. This has caused new poverty. Groups of vulnerable children in particular have been made to suffer: the girl child, the disabled, minority ethnic groups, orphans, displaced and refugee children.'[133]

---

[130] P. Parriaux, *The effect of structural adjustment programs on the potential of the poorest to cope with the drought in southern Africa*, Oxfam America, available on http://www.oxfamamerica.org/emergency/art3174.html.

[131] Report of the Independent Expert on the Effects on Structural Adjustment Policies and Foreign Debt, *Effects of Structural Adjustment Policies and Foreign Debt on the Full Enjoyment of Human Rights, Particularly Economic, Social and Cultural Rights* (UN Doc. E/CN.4/2003/10, 2002), para. 75 (c). The whole report reflects the position and analysis of the Independent Expert on the subject, including information on the position of UN agencies and NGOs, in addition to case studies.

[132] CRC Committee, *General Comment No. 5, o.c.* (note 39), para. 52.

[133] CRC Committee, *Day of General Discussion: Economic Exploitation of Children, 4th Session* (UN Doc. CRC/C/20,1993), Annex VI.

104. The UN Commission on Human Rights passed a resolution in 2001 on the effect of SAPs, which:

- '*Stresses* that structural adjustment policies have serious implications for the ability of the developing countries to abide by the Declaration on the Right to Development and to formulate national development policies that aim to improve the economic, social and cultural rights of their citizens;
- *Notes with concern* the persistence of the external debt problem, that the vicious cycle of debt and underdevelopment has become further entrenched, that debt service has grown at a much greater rate than the debt itself and that the burden of payments has become heavier in many developing countries, including those with low and middle incomes, despite repeated rescheduling, and that the current debt and poverty reduction and growth initiatives lack sufficient funding and have several conditions attached;
- *Recalls* the pledge, contained in the Political Declaration adopted by the General Assembly at its twenty-fourth special session, annexed to resolution S-24/2, of 1 July 2000, to find effective, equitable, development-oriented and durable solutions to the external debt and debt-servicing burdens of developing countries;
- *Reiterates* that the permanent solution to the foreign debt problem lies in the establishment of a just and equitable international economic order based, *inter alia*, in open, equitable, secure, non-discriminatory, predictable, transparent and multilateral rule-based international financial and trading systems, which guarantees the developing countries, *inter alia*, better market conditions and commodity prices, stabilization of exchange rates and interest rates, easier access to financial and capital markets, adequate flows of new financial resources and easier access to the technology of the developed countries.'[134]

105. This resolution undoubtedly reflects the serious nature of the problem, but also sets the agenda for what needs to be done in order to start resolving it. The emphasis on a 'just and equitable economic order' and what that entails should be the test for the success of any future financial programs for debt relief and international co-operation.

106. It is not yet clear what will be the impact of the new 'Heavily Indebted Poor Countries' initiative (HIPC), originally launched at the World Bank-IMF Annual meeting in 1996 and subsequently enhanced in 1999.[135] Similarly, the Poverty Reduction Strategy Papers (PRSPs), initiated by the IMF and the World Bank in 1999 are said to result 'in a comprehensive country-based

---

[134] Commission on Human Rights, *Resolution on the Effects of Structural Adjustment Policies and Foreign Debt on the Full Enjoyment of All Human Rights, Particularly Economic, Social and Cultural Rights* (Commission on Human Rights resolution 2001/27, 2001), paras. 2–5.

[135] According to the UN Independent Expert on SAPs it does 'mark a turning point in the global partnership to address one of the most serious problems in the developing world: debt sustainability. The goal of HIPC, as revised in 1999, is to ensure deep, broad and fast

strategy for poverty reduction. They aim to provide the crucial link between national public actions, donor support, and the development outcomes needed to meet the United Nations' Millennium Development Goals (MDGs) centered on halving poverty between 1990 and 2015.'[136] In the 'World Fit for Children' report, one of the targets adopted by the international community of States is to implement without further delay 'the enhanced Heavily Indebted Poor Countries Initiative and agree to cancel all bilateral official debts of heavily indebted poor countries as soon as possible, in return for demonstrable commitments by them to poverty eradication, and urge the use of debt service savings to finance poverty eradication programmes, in particular those related to children.'[137]

107. These two new initiatives have prompted diverse reactions by NGOs. Oxfam, for example, has declared that it 'supports civil society partners to engage in PRSP processes in 33 countries. Although the PRSP initiative is driven by the World Bank and the IMF, Oxfam believes that it offers a key opportunity to put country led strategies for poverty reduction at the heart of development assistance',[138] although it also notes that, unfortunately 'the promise of PRSPs' contribution to poverty reduction remains largely unfulfilled. Three years on, and over 50 PRSPs . . . later, a clear overall picture is emerging, based on our work with partners on PRSPs in more than thirty countries.'[139] On the other hand, commenting on these new policies and initiatives, Steve Tibbett, Head of the Policy department at War on Want says:

> 'This surely cannot be tolerated in the name of development. Trade negotiations and the distribution of aid by rich industrialised countries are tools of foreign policy used to further national self-interest.
> The developed model is the same as before: open your markets, increase your exports, privatize everything, liberalize your financial system and the rest will follow. Such fundamentalism elevates liberalization as an end in itself – the holy grail of economic progress.

---

debt relief with a strong link to poverty reduction. Recent global summits and international conferences, from the Millennium Summit to Monterrey and Johannesburg, have reaffirmed the importance of joint efforts of low-income, highly indebted developing countries and the concerted support by the international community, and the relevance of the HIPC initiative towards this end.' *Report Independent Expert on the Effects of Structural Adjustment Policies and Foreign Debt on the Full Enjoyment of All Human Rights, Particularly Economic, Social and Cultural Rights* (UN Doc. E/CN.4/2004/47, 2004), para. 7.

[136] IMF, *Fact Sheet on Poverty Reduction Strategy Papers*, available at: http://www.imf.org/external/np/exr/facts/prsp.htm.

[137] *A World Fit for Children, o.c.* (note 122), para. 52 (b).

[138] Oxfam, *Briefing Paper 51: Donorship to Ownership? Moving Towards PRSP Round Two*, available on http://www.oxfam.org.uk/what_we_do/issues/democracy_rights/bp51_prsp.htm.

[139] *Ibid.*

So we should not be fooled by the new outer casing – fluffy phrases such as 'ownership' 'partnership' and 'fighting poverty' are merely there to make the same bad medicine go down.'[140]

108. The CRC Committee has encouraged efforts to reduce poverty in the most heavily indebted countries through PRSPs whilst urging that in the framework of the central, country-led strategy for achieving the millennium development goals, PRSPs must include a strong focus on children's rights. The Committee urges Governments, donors and civil society to ensure that children are a prominent priority in the development of PRSPs and sectorwide approaches to development (SWAps). Both PRSPs and SWAps should reflect children's rights principles, with a holistic, child-centred approach recognizing children as holders of rights and the incorporation of development goals and objectives which are relevant to children.'[141]

109. The Committee has also stressed that the World Bank, IMF and the World Trade Organization should ensure that their international co-operation and economic development activities give primary consideration to the best interests of children and promote full implementation of the Convention. However, at the same time, the Committee has failed to urge Member States of these institutions to ensure that the CRC is at the centre of their activities.

4.3 *The Eight Millennium Development Goals (MDGs)*[142]

110. These were adopted at the Millennium Summit, and pledged to be met by UN Members by 2015. Several relate specifically to Children. For example, the second goal is to achieve universal primary education by ensuring that all boys and girls complete a full course of primary schooling, whilst the fourth is to reduce the child mortality rate among children under five by two thirds. The eighth, an over-arching goal to 'develop a global partnership for development', includes the target to 'develop decent and productive work for youth', in co-operation with the developing countries.

111. The language of these goals echo the language of the Commission on Human Rights Resolution 2001/27 cited above. However, it unfortunately

---

[140] 'The spoils of the war on poverty: The west's rhetoric about foreign aid conceals a greedy self-interest', *the Guardian*, 2 July 2003.

[141] CRC Committee, *General Comment No. 5, o.c.* (note 39), para. 62.

[142] A special web-page on the MDGs is available on the UN's main website on http://www.un.org/millenniumgoals/. Also a special web-page on the MDGs is available on the UNDP website on: http://www.undp.org/mdg/resources.html.

does not use the language related to international co-operation and the duty thereto as embodied in international human rights instruments as discussed above. In this context, it is interesting to note that the Draft Guidelines for Poverty Reduction consider international assistance and co-operation as the fifteenth right:

> 'The parameters of the right to international assistance and co-operation are not yet clearly drawn. However, in principle, it requires that all those in a position to assist should, first, refrain from acts that make it more difficult for the poor to realize their human rights and, second, take measures to remove obstacles that impede the realization by poor of their human rights. Thus, the right to international assistance and co-operation should not be understood as encompassing only financial and technical assistance: it also includes an obligation to work actively towards equitable multilateral trading, investment and financial systems that are conducive to the reduction and elimination of poverty.'[143]

112. This will therefore have an impact on children, as they often are the most marginalized and vulnerable members of society. Furthermore, given that different aspects of the above targets also relate to the other seven goals, there is a clear expectation that all of them are to be achieved through international co-operation, leading to the conclusion that this may be one of the most concrete ways of implementing the international co-operation dimension of Article 4. To implement the MDGs properly, responsible budgeting should ensure that resources are allocated to achieve each of the goals. Although the goals are broadly linked to poverty eradication., the term is not defined in a clear way. The UNDP Human Development Report in 1997 provides a useful human rights based definition, stating that poverty is 'the denial of opportunities and choices most basic to human development – to lead a long, healthy, creative life and enjoy a decent standard of living, freedom, dignity, self-esteem, and the respect for others.'[144] This definition reflects another main criticism of the MDGs by NGOs: that they are selective rather than inclusive, as they do not embrace many essential rights such as freedom from discrimination, or the right to food. Nor are they grounded in human rights terms. Although the MDGs are clearly linked to several economic or social rights and children's rights generally, their targets of achievements

---

[143] *Draft Guidelines: A Human Rights Approach to Poverty Reduction Strategies*, para. 216, found on http://www.unhchr.ch/development/povertyfinal.html#guid4. These are the outcome of the request by the CESCR Committee in 2001 to the OHCHR to develop substantive guidelines for the integration of human rights in national poverty reduction strategies.

[144] UNDP, *1997 Human Development Report: Human Development To Eradicate Poverty*, available at http://hdr.undp.org/reports/global/1997/en/.

are not presented in terms of rights and corresponding obligations under international law. Furthermore, the fact that the goals are broadly linked to progressive realization does not make it clear whether in practice this would mean realization to the 'maximum extent of available resources', as required by both the CRC and CESCR, or whether it would be sufficient for a State to demonstrate that it is moving forward towards achieving the goals, but not necessarily to the maximum of its available resources.[145] This issue has been addressed by both the CESCR Committee and the various special rapporteurs on economic, social and cultural rights (housing, education, health) when they issued a statement urging that '[e]conomic, social and cultural rights should be the criteria when establishing tools for measuring progress towards the achievement of MDGs' and that '[t]he concepts of progressive realization and resource availability enshrined in the CESCR are important guidelines of any strategy which aims at meeting the MDGs.'[146]

5. Reservations

113. Article 19 (3) of the Viena Convention on the Law of Treaties provides the possibility for States to make a reservation at the time of ratification or accession to a treaty, unless it is incompatible with the object and purpose of the treaty. This principle is reflected in Article 51 (2) of the CRC which states: 'A reservation incompatible with the object and purpose of the present Convention shall not be permitted.'[147] There are no specific reservations that have been entered to Article 4 of the CRC.[148] However, it should be recognized that, given the all embracing nature of the provision, reservations

---

[145] For a discussion on the MDGs from a human rights perspective, see Centre for Human Rights and Global Justice, *Human Rights Perspective on the Millennium Goals: Conference Report* (New York, NYU School of Law, 2003).

[146] *A Joint Statement by the UN Committee on Economic, Social and Cultural Rights and the UN Commission on Human Rights' Special Rapporteurs on Economic, Social and Cultural Rights* (29 November 2002), para. 5.

[147] The Human Rights Committee adds: 'Reservations that offend peremptory norms would not be compatible with the object and purpose of the Covenant. Although treaties that are mere exchanges of obligations between States allow them to reserve *inter se* application of rules of general international law, it is otherwise in human rights treaties, which are for the benefit of persons within their jurisdiction. Accordingly, provisions in the Covenant that represent customary international law (and *a fortiori* when they have the character of peremptory norms) may not be the subject of reservations.' See Human Rights Committee, *General Comment No. 24: Issues Relating to Reservations Made Upon Ratification or Accession to the Covenant or the Optional Protocols Thereto, or in Relation to Declarations Under Article 41 of the Covenant* (UN Doc. CCPR/C/21/Rev.1/Add.6, 1994), para. 8.

[148] For a full text of reservations entered to the CRC, see http://www.ohchr.org/english/countries/ratification/11.htm#reservations.

entered to other articles in the CRC have the potential of also undermining its implementation.

114. There are generally three types of reservations entered to the CRC: those made because the provisions of the Convention conflict with national legislation, those entered because of conflict with religious law, particularly the Islamic Shari'a, or a combination of both.

5.1 Reservations Due to Conflict with National Legislation

115. Tunisia, for example, made a declaration when it ratified the CRC stating that 'it shall not, in implementation of this Convention, adopt any legislative or statutory decision that conflicts with the Tunisian Constitution.' A similar reservation has been made by Botswana when it made a reservation to Article 1 'so far as such may conflict with the Laws and Statutes of Botswana.'[149] The Government of the former Federal Republic of Germany objected to the declaration by Tunisia, stating that: 'Owing to the very general wording of this passage, the Government of the Federal Republic of Germany is unable to perceive which provisions of the Convention are covered, or may be covered at some time in the future, by the reservation and in what manner. There is a similar lack of clarity with regard to the reservation relating to Article 2.'[150]

116. This approach is further reinforced by Article 27 of the Vienna Convention on the Law of Treaties when it provides that '[a] party may not invoke the provisions of its internal law as justification for its failure to perform a treaty.' Similarly, the Human Rights Committee expressed its particular concern about the 'widely formulated reservations which essentially render ineffective all [CCPR] rights requiring any change in national law to ensure compliance with Covenant obligations. No real international rights or obligations have thus been accepted.'[151] It is therefore clear that a State should not invoke national legislation as a pretext for not implementing its obligations of the CRC. Otherwise, ratification of the CRC and making an

---

[149] As the Human Rights Committee observes: 'It is not always easy to distinguish a reservation from a declaration as to a State's understanding of the interpretation of a provision, or from a statement of policy. Regard will be had to the intention of the State, rather than the form of the instrument. If a statement, irrespective of its name or title, purports to exclude or modify the legal effect of a treaty in its application to the State, it constitutes a reservation.' See Human Rights Committee, *General Comment No. 24*, o.c. (note 147), para. 3.

[150] See text of the reservation of Tunisia and the objection of Germany on http://www.ohchr.org/english/countries/ratification/11.htm#reservations.

[151] Human Rights Committee, *General Comment No. 24, o.c.* (note 147), para. 12.

undertaking according to Article 4 to introduce all appropriate legislative measures becomes meaningless. Instead, 'taking such legislative measures' means that national legislation should be amended to reflect the principles and provisions of the CRC, rather than limiting the implementation of the Convention because the national legislation does not reflect these provisions or principles.

5.2   Reservations Due to Conflict with Islamic Shari'a

117. The Governments of Saudi Arabia and Iran entered a general reservation to the CRC 'with respect to all such articles as are in conflict with the provisions of Islamic law.'[152] Other States have entered similar reservations in relation to specific provisions, for example, the United Arab Emirates in relation to Article 14 (freedom of expression).[153] It should be noted that Egypt had entered a specific reservation to Articles 20 and 21 (in relation to adoption), but this was lifted on 31 July 2003.[154] This was the only country so far to lift such reservations due to conflict with Islamic law.

118. The fact that not all the countries which have Islamic Shari'a as a source, or the sole basis, for legislation have made such sweeping reservations, reflects that there are different interpretations as to what constitutes being in conflict with Shari'a law. In this respect, the lifting of the reservation by Egypt is significant, because it shows that there are different interpretations regarding this issue and that interpretations are not, and should not be static, but can be subject to change. Recently, the CRC Committee has expressed its deep regret that in the Islamic republic of Iran, no review has been undertaken of the broad and imprecise nature of the State Party's reservation since the presentation of the initial report. It reiterates its concern that the nature of the general reservation potentially negates many of the Convention's provisions and raises concern as to its compatibility with the object and purpose of the Convention. It calls on the State Party to 'review the general nature of its reservation with a view to withdrawing it, or narrowing it.'[155]

---

[152] See http://www.ohchr.org/english/countries/ratification/11.htm#reservations.
[153] *Ibid.*
[154] *Ibid.*
[155] CRC Committee, *Concluding Observations*: Iran (UN Doc. CRC/C/15/Add.254, 2005), paras. 6 and 7.

5.3   Reservations Due to Conflict with Islamic Shari'a and National Legislation

119. Afghanistan, Kuwait, and Syria have made general reservations to all provisions of the Convention that are incompatible with the laws of Islamic Shari'a and the local legislation.[156] In addition to this general reservation, Syria has specified reservations to Articles 14 (concerning freedom of religion), and Articles 20 and 21 (concerning adoption). In doing so, these States have subjected the provisions of the CRC to maximum restrictions and very narrow interpretation.

5.4   Lifting Reservations

120. It is unfortunate that the CRC Committee did not call clearly in General Comment No. 5 for the lifting of the reservations that are contrary to the purpose and objects of the Convention. However, the Committee has expressed its deep concern 'that some States have made reservations which plainly breach Article 51 (2) by suggesting, for example, that respect for the Convention is limited by the State's existing constitution or legislation, including in some cases religious law.'[157]

121. The CRC Committee requires that a State should report on whether it considers it necessary to maintain the reservations it has made, or has the intention of withdrawing them. The reporting on this falls under the 'General Measures of Implementation' of the Reporting Guidelines of the Committee, which includes reporting on Article 4 of the CRC.[158] In general, the Committee has recommended during its examination of reports that reservations be reviewed and withdrawn, and if a State Party decides to maintain a reservation, it should include a full explanation in its next periodic report.[159] A clear statement in its General Comment that is consistent with the Committee's own practice would have had an important effect on governments to lift at least those reservations that are not consistent with the purpose and object of the CRC, and to review their reservations and take measures to lift other reservations. The Vienna Declaration and Plan of Action made a clearer recommendation when it stated that: 'The World

---

[156] See text of reservations on http://www.ohchr.org/english/countries/ratification/11.htm #reservations.

[157] CRC Committee, *General Comment No. 5, o.c.* (note 39), para. 15.

[158] CRC Committee, *General Guidelines Regarding the Form and Content of Periodic Reports, o.c.* (note 56), para. 11.

[159] See further on this CRC Committee, *General Comment No. 5, o.c.* (note 39), para. 13.

Conference on Human Rights urges States to withdraw reservations to the Convention on the Rights of the Child contrary to the object and purpose of the Convention or otherwise contrary to international law.'[160]

6. *Implementation*

122. This section will not include a review of the role of the CRC Committee in monitoring implementation of the Convention, but rather on general implementation aspects, focusing particularly on the issues of review and evaluation, domestic remedies and on ways to measure progress in the implementation of economic, social and cultural rights.

6.1 *Review and Evaluation*

123. Ensuring effective implementation of the CRC requires putting measures in place which enable periodic review of progress made. This process should ideally involve different government agencies, as well as the non-governmental sector, particularly NGOs working for and with children. The submission of reports to the CRC Committee on measures of implementation, progress achieved and difficulties faced gives States Parties the opportunity to revisit their programs periodically. The CRC Committee recommends that there should be 'a continuous process of child impact assessment (predicting the impact of any proposed law, policy or budgetary allocation which affects children and the enjoyment of their rights) and child impact evaluation (evaluating the actual impact of implementation).'[161] While monitoring implementation is the primary task of the government, such monitoring can be carried out by other bodies, including NGOs, Parliament, and other institutions. It is essential for the government to benefit from such independent reviews and evaluation and engage in a positive dialogue with all those concerned parties in order to identify errors or difficulties and ways of overcoming them. It is also essential in this context that the voices of the children are heard since they are best placed to express how their rights have been violated (or not implemented).[162]

---

[160] Vienna Declaration and Plan of Action, para. 46.

[161] CRC Committee, *General Comment No. 5, o.c.* (note 39), para. 45.

[162] Article 12 (1) of the CRC provides that 'States Parties shall assure to the child who is capable of forming his or her own views the right to express those views freely in all matters affecting the child, the views of the child being given due weight in accordance with the age and maturity of the child.' See X., 'Participation: The Missing P in the Convention on the Rights of the Child', *INTERIGHTS Bulletin* Vol. 14(2), 2003.

124. An example of this holistic approach can be found in the CRC Committee's General Comment No 5, concurring with paragraph 42 of General Comment No. 14 of the CESCR on the right to the highest attainable standard of health, when it states that: 'While only States are Parties to the Covenant and thus ultimately accountable for compliance with it, all members of society – individuals, including health professionals, families, local communities, intergovernmental and non-governmental organizations, civil society organizations, as well as the private business sector – have responsibilities regarding the realization of the right to health. States Parties should therefore provide an environment which facilitates the discharge of these responsibilities.'[163] This highlights the importance of involving civil society in all stages of implementation, including policy-making and evaluation, particularly where it is acting as a provider of services. The CRC Committee also believes that there is an important role for NGOs in the monitoring process of the CRC. For example, the conclusions adopted by the Committee on the occasion of the tenth anniversary of the CRC state:

> 'The Committee encourages non-governmental organizations, and legal professionals and scholars, to give priority attention to providing legal analysis of existing legislation and its compatibility with the Convention to the Committee, so they can be of use in its examination of reports presented by States Parties. . . .'[164]

6.2   Effective Remedy

125. Ensuring an effective remedy is an integral part of the implementation of any human rights treaty and this has been emphasized by the CRC Committee:

> 'States need to give particular attention to ensuring that there are effective, child-sensitive procedures available to children and their representatives. These should include the provision of child-friendly information, advice, advocacy, including support for self-advocacy, and access to independent complaints procedures and to the courts with necessary legal and other assistance. Where rights are found to have been breached, there should be appropriate reparation, including compensation, and, where needed, measures to promote physical and psychological recovery, rehabilitation and reintegration.'[165]

---

[163] CESCR Committee, *General Comment No. 14, o.c.* (note 91), para. 42. The CRC Committee supported this in its General Comment No. 5, *o.c.* (note 39), para. 56.
[164] CRC Committee, *Report on the twenty-first session, o.c.* (note 102), p. 94, para. G.
[165] CRC Committee, *General Comment No. 5, o.c.* (note 39), para. 24.

126. Of course, given that the right to an effective remedy is enshrined in other international human rights treaties,[166] the obligations on the State to make these remedies available to children also exists under these other instruments. What is missing is how to make these remedies child-friendly in line with Article 3 (1) of the CRC which states: 'In all actions concerning children, whether undertaken by public or private social welfare institutions, courts of law, administrative authorities or legislative bodies, the best interests of the child shall be a primary consideration.' To facilitate this principle, the Committee has recommended that States Parties establish an independent national human rights institution, in accordance with the Paris Principles Relating to the Status of National Institutions (General Assembly resolution 48/134) to monitor and evaluate progress in the implementation of the Convention at the national and local levels. This institution should be empowered to receive and investigate complaints of violations of child rights in a child-friendly manner, and address them effectively.[167]

127. Effective remedies include accessible mechanisms of complaint, as well as prompt, independent, and impartial mechanisms of investigations into claims of violations. It also includes the right to reparation, including restitution, compensation, and rehabilitation. In addition, there must be ways to implement provisional or interim measures to avoid continuing violations and to endeavour to repair at the earliest possible any harm that may have been caused by such violations.

6.3 *Administrative Measures*

128. The Committee expects to see that 'the Convention must be reflected in professional training curricula, codes of conduct and educational curricula at all levels, stressing that understanding and knowledge of human rights must, of course, be promoted among children themselves, including through the school curriculum.'[168]

129. Further, it is essential that children's rights and concerns are incorporated in the government at all levels. As the Committee has stated, 'virtually all government departments' impact on children's lives. It is not

---

[166] See for example Article 2 (3a) of the CCPR, Article 6 of the CERD and Articles 12, 13 and 14 of the CAT.
[167] CRC Committee, *Concluding Observations*: Saudi Arabia (UN Doc. CRC/C/15/Add.148, 2001), para. 18.
[168] CRC Committee, *General Comment No. 5, o.c.* (note 39), para. 53.

practicable to bring responsibility for all children's services together into a single department, and in any case doing so could have the danger of further marginalizing children in Government. But a special unit, if given high-level authority – reporting directly, for example, to the Prime Minister, the President or a Cabinet Committee on children – can contribute both to the overall purpose of making children more visible in Government and of co-ordinating to ensure respect for children's rights across Government and at all levels of Government.'[169] The Committee has in some cases recommended that there should be a focal point for children within the government, and in other occasions welcomed the establishment of an inter-ministerial committee on children.[170] The Committee has also referred to lack of coordination between different governmental departments and ministries, and with the civil society and NGOs, and requested that such coordination should be ensured.[171]

6.4 *Use of Data and Indicators*

130. In order to effectively monitor the implementation of the CRC, the Committee has always required detailed disaggregated statistical data covering *inter alia* gender, age, race, national origin, place of residence, and family status. In its General Guidelines for periodic reports, for example, the Committee asks States Parties to provide information 'using indicators or target figures where necessary, [to] indicate the measures undertaken to ensure the implementation at the national, regional and local levels, and where relevant at the federal and provincial levels, of the economic, social and cultural rights of children to the maximum extent of available resources.'[172] Such data need to be disaggregated in terms of not just gender and age, but also geography, ethnicity and religion, in order to determine if there is discrimination against any of these sectors in either policies or practice, and if 'data collection needs to extend over the whole period of childhood, up to the age of 18 years. It also needs to be coordinated throughout the jurisdiction, ensuring nationally applicable indicators. States should collaborate with appropriate research institutes and aim to build up a complete picture of progress towards implementation, with qualitative as well as quantitative studies.'[173]

---

[169] *Ibid.*, para. 39.
[170] See R. Hodgkin and P. Newell, *o.c.* (note 1), p. 68.
[171] *Ibid.*, pp. 69–70.
[172] CRC Committee, *General Guidelines Regarding the Form and Content of Periodic Reports, o.c.* (note 56), para. 20.
[173] CRC Committee, *General Comment No. 5, o.c.* (note 39), para. 48.

131. It is essential to ensure that the data collected are evaluated and used to assess progress in implementation, to identify problems and to inform policy development. It is therefore important to ensure that there are mechanisms to collect and review data periodically. Data should be made available to and used by various sectors in the government, including the relevant ministries and departments in the government, by the parliament and by NGOs. The CRC Committee places great emphasis on interviewing children, or even using children as researchers to collect data, thereby ensuring that children are visible in the data, and that their concerns are adequately reflected. [174]

132. The CRC Committee, when reviewing States Parties' reports, relies also on information and data provided by UN agencies. Several of these agencies have developed sophisticated methodologies for collecting data and, as a result, have extensive data sets in relation to many rights, for example, WHO in relation to health, UNAIDS in relation to HIV/AIDS and the ILO in relation to child labour. It goes without saying that UNICEF has access to key data in relation to children across many sectors. Agencies have also developed rights centred indicators which are used to set appropriate targets in order to fulfil the respective rights. It is very important that this data is used by States regularly as part of their periodic reviews of policies and measures.

133. Given that all human rights treaties, including the CRC, place obligations on governments to implement rights, it is important to determine their *willingness* and/or the *ability* to carry out these obligations.[175] Indicators are required to measure the degree of commitment to human rights reflecting the progressive, or regressive realization of both sets of rights, for example, on registration of children after birth (*i.e.* to ensure access to education and nationality rights) or access to free compulsory primary education. Such indicators should not take only the form of segregated data, but also include whether there are appropriate laws in place, or institutions created and supported to implement the rights in question.[176]

---

[174] *Ibid.*, para. 50.
[175] Maastricht Guidelines, para. 13.
[176] A thorough discussion of indicators is beyond the scope of this paper. For further discussion on the subject, see: K. Tomasevski, 'Indicators', in A. Eide, C. Krause and A. Rosas (eds.), *Economic, social and Cultural Rights, Second revised Edition*, (Dordrecht/Boston/London, Martinus Nijhoff Publishers, 2001), pp. 531–544.

134. But the main question remains how this data and indicators can be used to determine if a violation of economic, social and cultural rights in the CRC has occurred. The views of the CESCR Committee are helpful in this regard. The CESCR Committee is of the view that a minimum core obligation is incumbent on every State Party in order to ensure the satisfaction of, at the very least, a minimum essential level of each of the rights. Further, the Committee adds that in order for a State Party to be able to attribute its failure to meet at least its minimum core obligations to a lack of available resources it must demonstrate that every effort has been made to use all resources that are at its disposition in an effort to satisfy, as a matter of priority, those minimum obligations.'[177] Therefore, data and indicators could assist in demonstrating whether indeed all resources at the disposition of the State Party have been used in an attempt to fulfil its obligations under Article 4 of the CRC.

135. A good example of the interlink between indicators and benchmarks, and the need for regular assessment is found in the Draft Guidelines for a Human Rights Approach to Poverty Reduction Strategies. According to this document, plans for poverty reduction 'must include a series of intermediate – preferably annual – targets. As the realization of human rights may take some considerable time, possibly extending well beyond the immediate term of a Government in power, it is with regard to these intermediate targets (or benchmarks) rather than the final target of full realization that the State will have to be held accountable.' The Guidelines add that it is a prerequisite of setting targets that the State in question 'will have to identify some indicators in terms of which targets will be set. In practice, a bundle of indicators will be needed for each human right, and they should be specified separately, at levels that are as disaggregated, as far as possible, for each subgroup of the poor population. Realistic time-bound targets will have to be set in relation to each indicator so as to serve as benchmarks.' The draft Guidelines include useful indicators on poverty reduction in relation to rights to adequate food, health, education, decent work, adequate housing, personal security, equal access to justice, political rights and freedoms and what the Draft Guidelines term 'appearance in public without shame.' The Guidelines demonstrate the indivisibility of rights by requiring that clear goals and targets related to civil, political, economic, and social rights are included in country strategies for poverty reduction.

---

[177] CESCR Committee, *General Comment No. 3, o.c.* (note 80), para. 10.

136. However, the difficulty remains how to determine what the minimum core obligations are and whether a State has in fact used its maximum available resources. It has been pointed out that the concept is possibly one of the most difficult to realize in terms of economic, social and cultural rights since it aims to bridge the gap between the goals and the available resources.[178] A clearer interpretation of what these obligations are has begun to be provided by the CESCR Committee in its recent General Comments.[179] In the General Comments, the normative content of the right is explained, followed by an elaboration of the nature of the obligations and violations. The General Comments focus on elaborating the obligations to *respect, protect and fulfil* each of the rights concerned. The obligation to *respect* requires States to refrain from interfering directly or indirectly with the enjoyment of the right; the obligation to *protect* requires States to take measures that prevent third parties from interfering with the right in question; and the obligation to *fulfil* contains obligations to facilitate, provide and promote as well as adopt appropriate legislative, administrative, budgetary, judicial, promotional and other measures towards the full realization of the right in question.[180] The last two General Comments on the Right to the Highest Attainable Standard of Health and the Right to Water specify the minimum core content and obligation of each of the concerned rights. The previous others include some useful commentary on the core content of the concerned rights. The African Commission on Human Rights has added to this typology the obligation to *promote*.[181]

137. The violations approach to economic, social and cultural rights, proposed first by Audrey Chapman and elaborated in both the Limburg Principles and the Maastricht Guidelines provide a very useful guidance on how to determine

---

[178] See A. Chapman and S. Russell (eds), *Core Obligations: Building a Framework for Economic, Social and Cultural Rights* (Antwerp/Oxford/New York, Intersentia, 2002), 351 pp. The book uses the concept of core obligations to analyse several economic, social and cultural rights. The introduction of the book provides a useful overview of the concept.

[179] See CESCR Committee, *General Comment No. 11: Plans of Action for Primary Education* (UN Doc. E/C.12/1999/4, 1999), *General Comment No. 12: The Right to Adequate Food* (UN Doc. E/C.12/1999/5, 1999), *General Comment No. 13: The Right to Education* (UN Doc. E/C.12/1999/10, 1999), *General Comment No. 14, o.c.* (note 91), and *General Comment No. 15: The Right to Water* (E/C.12/2002/11, 2002).

[180] CESCR Committee, *General Comment No. 14, o.c.* (note 91), para. 33.

[181] See African Commission on Human Rights, *The Social and Economic Rights Action Centre and the Centre for Economic and Social Rights v. Nigeria*, ACHPR/COMM/A044/1, 27 May 2002, para. 44.

violations of these rights. It is proposed that violations of economic, social and cultural rights occur when the State fails to take steps required, or to remove obstacles, or to implement without delay a certain right required by international instruments to be provided immediately, or wilfully fails to meet internationally accepted standards, or applies limitations to rights in a way not consistent with international standards, or it deliberately retards or halts progressive realization, or finally it fails to submit reports to the relevant treaty bodies.[182]

138. It is unfortunate that the CRC Committee in its General Comment No. 5 on General Measures of Implementation of the CRC did not use this methodology developed by the CESCR Committee. It is hoped that the CRC Committee will elaborate on this area in future general comments on specific rights.

---

[182] See A. Chapman, 'A "Violations Approach" for Monitoring the International Covenant on Economic, Social and Cultural Rights', *Human Rights Quarterly* 18, 1996, pp. 23–66.

CHAPTER FOUR

CONCLUSIONS

139. Article 4 of the CRC enables State obligations in relation to the Convention to be viewed in a holistic and comprehensive way. The CRC was drafted after a host of other human rights treaties had been adopted and widely ratified. Therefore, the drafting of the CRC, and its interpretation has benefited from interpretations and lessons learnt from the other previous treaties. Because of the close similarity between Article 4 and other articles in other international and regional human rights treaties, the nature of State obligations should be interpreted in the light of not only the development of the jurisprudence of the CRC Committee, but that of other treaty bodies and regional mechanisms. This is reinforced by the very specific recommendations made by the CRC Committee on measures that can be taken to implement the CRC. The Committee's General Comment No. 5 on General Measures of Implementation of the CRC draws not only on the Committee's own past experience, but also other treaty bodies and UN fora, providing the basis for concrete programming and drawing up of policies by States Parties in relation to children's rights.

140. In addition, the concluding observations issued by the CRC Committee and other relevant bodies when reviewing States Parties' reports result in very specific country recommendations. If followed by States and monitored by appropriate national mechanisms, they should enable States to progress towards full realization of their obligations in line with Article 4. This requires that States also co-operate with the respective treaty bodies in relation to submission of reports in the first place.

141. Ultimately, Article 4 cuts across all the rights in the CRC and it is vital that their implementation is carried out in the light of Article 4. Adequate attention given to the implementation of Article 4 of the CRC would necessarily lead to advancing the implementation of obligations in relation to other rights. The implementation of Article 4, which is at the heart of States Parties' obligations, requires that detailed plans are made, and attention is given to evaluation of plans, review of legislation, assessing ways of measuring progress, as well involving various sectors in the planning and implementation process.